LRUZ

the war
over
iraq

the war over iraq

Saddam's Tyranny and America's Mission

LAWRENCE F. KAPLAN
WILLIAM KRISTOL

ENCOUNTER BOOKS
SAN FRANCISCO, CALIFORNIA

Copyright © 2003 by Lawrence F. Kaplan and William Kristol

Published by Encounter Books, an activity of Encounter for Culture and Education, Inc., a nonprofit tax exempt corporation.

Encounter Books website address: www.encounterbooks.com

Manufactured in the United States and printed on acid-free paper.

The paper used in this publication meets the minimum requirements of ANSI/NISO Z39.48-1992 (R 1997)(*Permanence of Paper*).

FIRST EDITION

Library of Congress Cataloging-in-Publication Data

Kaplan, Lawrence F., 1969–
    The war over iraq : Saddam's tyranny and America's mission / Lawrence F. Kaplan and William Kristol.
       p.   cm.
       Includes bibliographic references and index.
       ISBN 1-893554-69-4 (alk. paper)
       1.   Hussein, Saddam, 1937–.   2.   United States—Foreign relations—Iraq.   3.   Iraq—Foreign relations—United States.   4.   United States—Foreign relations—1989–.   5.   Iraq—Foreign relations—1979–1991.   6.   Iraq—Foreign relations—1991–.   7.   United States—Military policy.   I.   Kristol, William.
    II. Title.
    E183.8.I57 K75 2003
    327.730567—dc21

                                                                            2003040784

10   9   8   7   6   5   4

Contents

Introduction

After four decades of cold war, and a decade of relative peace and prosperity, we stand at the cusp of a new historical era. Neither forty years of confrontation with the Soviet Union nor the decade-long sigh of relief after its fall prepared us particularly well for this moment. For all the arenas in which it was fought and the moments of high drama that marked its history, the Cold War—as metaphors like containment and the Iron Curtain suggest—presented an essentially static challenge for American foreign policy. We thought it would always be with us. And when we found during the 1990s that it no longer was, we took a holiday from history, presuming that we could rely on commerce and globalization to achieve peace and stability. But the complacent assumptions of the post–Cold War era were destroyed on September 11. That day brought us to a new era, for which we need a new roadmap.

The new era is fluid, perilous and very much subject to the contingencies of history that define those moments when one epoch has died and another is struggling to be born. If America does not shape this new epoch, we can be sure that others will shape it for us—in ways that neither further our interests nor reflect our ideals. For the United States, then, this is a decisive moment. During the Cold War, Americans made choices in places like Berlin and Korea whose implications continued to resonate for decades. Now we face decisions of similar weight and consequence in places like Afghanistan and, most of all, Iraq.

The decision about what course to take in dealing with Iraq is particularly significant because it is so clearly about more than Iraq. It is about more even than the future of the Middle East and the war on terror. It is about what sort of role the United States intends to play in the world in the twenty-first century. And it is about what sort of a world Americans intend to inhabit—a world of civilized norms that is congenial to the United States, or a world where dictators feel no constraints about developing weapons of mass destruction at home and no compunction about committing aggression and supporting terrorism abroad. Hence, the reasons for choosing war against Saddam and the lessons we draw from this war will be as momentous as the choice itself. We believe it is vital to liberate Iraq and to liberate ourselves from the dangers that Iraq presents. But we also believe that the principles that have persuaded the Bush administration to pursue this course should guide our foreign policy more broadly. That is the argument of this book.

Iraq has been the arena in which competing American approaches to foreign policy have been most visible in the last decade, and most visibly put to the test. The three post–Cold War U.S. presidencies have possessed distinctive worldviews, each of which has been epitomized by how that administration has dealt with Iraq. And today the challenge that Saddam Hussein poses has forced the United States to clarify its practical objectives and moral obligations in the world.

Guided by a narrow *realpolitik* that defined America's vital interests in terms of oil wells, strategic chokepoints and regional stability, the first Bush administration halted its war against Saddam after expelling his armies from Kuwait. It then abandoned tens of thousands of Iraqis whom the United States had encouraged to rise up against Saddam, leaving him in power to bedevil us, and his own people, for the next decade. Then came the Clinton administration, which subscribed to a post-Vietnam brand of wishful liberalism that led it to recoil from the serious and sustained assertion of American power. The one worldview regarded Iraq as little more than a move on a diplomatic board game. The other responded to Saddam's provocations with bouts of hand-wringing, with occasional pinprick missile attacks, or by simply ignoring them.

Until recently, the record of American policy toward Iraq has mostly been one of failure; but Iraq can now provide a model for success. Having broken with the record of his predecessors, President George W. Bush brings to the problem of Iraq a worldview that reflects what he describes as "the union of our values and our national interests." With his history of aggression abroad and tyranny at home, Saddam Hussein is an affront to both. Thus, the president does not speak of merely containing or disarming Iraq, as his predecessors did. Instead, he speaks of liberating Iraq, and creating democracy in a land that for decades has known only dictatorship. In short, President Bush speaks of engaging Iraq in accord with American principles.

This will strike many as a tall order—but not nearly so tall as the president's insistence on engaging *the world* in accord with American principles. In his speeches, in his national security strategy, and in the doctrine named after him, President Bush not only demands that the United States dissuade potential adversaries from seeking to compete with the military might of the United States. The president also speaks bluntly of exporting the American creed "in keeping with our heritage and principles," which will in turn "create a balance of power that favors human freedom." By enshrining in official policy the tactic of military preemption, the objective of regime change and a vision of American power that is fully engaged and never apologetic, the Bush administration hopes to accomplish this happy end. We think it can. In the aftermath of September 11, we think it must.

The War over Iraq wears its heart on its sleeve. In arguing for the liberation of Iraq, we try to make the case for war honestly and straightforwardly, so the debate can be joined. We present a detailed account of Saddam's evil; a critical history of America's policies toward Iraq and a description of the competing philosophies that animated those policies; an analysis of the Bush Doctrine; and an argument for making that doctrine the basis of American foreign policy. *The War over Iraq* looks back at how a brutal dictator was allowed to acquire so much power on the world stage. But it also offers a roadmap for a more hopeful future. The wisdom of regime change, the merits of promoting democracy, the desirability of American power and influence—these issues extend well beyond Iraq. So we dare to hope that this work will prove useful even after Baghdad is finally free.

To cover so much ground, we have relied on dozens of books and hundreds of articles that have been written about Iraq, and more generally about American foreign policy. For accounts of Saddam Hussein's crimes, we benefited greatly from the following indispensable works: *Saddam Hussein and the Crisis in the Gulf,* by Judith Miller and Laurie Mylroie; *Republic of Fear,* by Kanan Makiya; *The Reckoning,* by Sandra Mackey; and *With Friends Like These,* by Bruce Jentleson. For a somewhat different argument from ours in favor of invading Iraq, we would refer readers to Kenneth Pollack's recent *The Threatening Storm.* We draw in this book from articles that Kaplan penned for the *New Republic,* and thank Laura Obolensky of the *New Republic* for permission to do so; from one article by Kristol in the *Weekly Standard;* and from an essay by Kristol and Robert Kagan in the volume they edited, *Present Dangers.*

We also relied heavily on the assistance of a few very able researchers. Chief among them is Daniel McKivergan of the Project for a New American Century, along with Christopher Maletz, also of the Project, and Reihan Salam of the Council on Foreign Relations. We could not have completed this book without their aid. Elianna Marziani, Cheryl Miller and Monica Tarantino of the Project for the New American Century also provided crucial assistance for which we are grateful. Katherine Mangu-Ward of the *Weekly Standard* contributed the index with speed and good cheer.

The idea for this book originated with two friends and colleagues: Gary Schmitt, director of the Project for a New American Century, and Peter Collier, president of Encounter Books. Both have been invaluable in seeing this project through from beginning to end, and in everything from helping us think through big questions to correcting errors and improving prose. We are most grateful to them both. We also would like to thank Carolyn Wimmer of the *Weekly Standard* for her important assistance.

Lawrence F. Kaplan would like to thank Peter Beinart, editor of the *New Republic,* for granting him a generous leave and for reminding him why *TNR* is home. His friends and mentors Andrew Bacevich and Joshua Muravchik provided wisdom and encouragement. Donald and Gail Liscomb, John and Patricia Meaney, Betty Edmiston, Joan Busner and Stuart Kaplan all offered helping hands. As always, Sandra Kaplan offered even more, and as always, he is extremely grateful. No amount of gratitude and affection can repay Sarah Meaney, who consoled, encouraged and kept Lawrence afloat during the writing of this book.

Saddam's Tyranny

ONE

Tyranny at Home

Of all the adjectives that George W. Bush has used during his two years in office, none has elicited more howls of derision than the four-letter word "evil." Just as Ronald Reagan was condemned for characterizing the Soviet Union as evil, a chorus of leading opinion makers has lampooned Bush for applying the same term to America's new foes. But as the events of 9-11 remind us, evil exists in this world, and it has consequences. Fortunately, evil can be defeated. Just as Ronald Reagan's assault on the "evil empire" was key to toppling Soviet communism, so has President Bush's response to the evil of September 11 exacted a steep price from the terrorists who orchestrated that horrible day.

As well as provoking a military response from the United States, September 11 prompted the president to identify an "axis of evil." It consists of regimes whose records of aggression, inventories of deadly weapons and support for terrorism pose a threat to the United States and the rest of the world. Chief among them is Iraq under the brutal rule of Saddam Hussein.

The more one learns about the Iraqi dictator, the clearer it becomes that he epitomizes—no less than Osama bin Laden—sheer malice. Here, after all, is a man who has imposed a violent, totalitarian regime on the people of Iraq. He has imprisoned, tortured, gassed, shot and bombed thousands upon thousands of his own subjects. He has launched wars of aggression against several of his neighbors, and still seeks to dominate the Middle East. He has expended vast resources on the development of an arsenal of weapons of mass destruction. He is at once a tyrant, an aggressor and, in his own avowed objectives, a threat to civilization.

3

Alas, for many in the West, Saddam's misdeeds seem not to have made much of an impression. From Europe, whose countries have supplied Baghdad with much of its deadly inventory and still seek to do business there, cynicism is perhaps to be expected. From China, a dictatorship in its own right, indifference hardly comes as a shock. And from the Arab countries, whose regimes are concerned with their own grip on power, an aversion to change is no surprise. Even in the United States, however, where 9-11 should have prompted a special vigilance, there has been complacency. The debate over war with Iraq has shown that too many opinion makers, elected officials and others who guide the fortunes of the world's sole superpower have lost their capacity to identify evil and to act against it. Even when it stares them in the face.

The tyrant whose depredations so many hesitate to interrupt came into the world on April 28, 1937. The future dictator was born near the town of Tikrit, in a poor village consisting largely of mud huts. Saddam's birth, recounts one of his official biographers, "was not a joyful occasion, and no roses or aromatic plants bedecked his cradle." Iraqi accounts gloss over the details of his youth, except to say that he claims descent from the prophet Muhammad. Western sources claim that Saddam's father either died or left his mother before Saddam was born. For their part, his former classmates remember that young Saddam was a bully who, among other things, carried a gun to school. But this much at least is clear: Saddam's uncle, Khayrallah Tulfah, took him under his wing at an early age, bringing him from his native Tikrit to Baghdad. Tulfah was a coup plotter whose political leanings reflected the agenda of the Iraqi Baath Party. He tutored the young Saddam in the blend of socialism, fascism and pan-Arab nationalism that distinguished Baathist politics. (A pamphlet that Tulfah authored, "Three Whom God Should Not Have Created: Persians, Jews and Flies," captures the flavor of his views.) As a teenager, Saddam followed in his uncle's footsteps, attending Baath cell meetings, engaging in street battles with university students, and spending nearly as much time in prison as out.

His political education complete, at the tender age of twenty-two, Saddam attempted but failed to gun down the prime minister of Iraq, Abdul Karim Kassim. "Wounded during the incident by the fire of one of his comrades," one of Saddam's official biographies boasts, "he extracted, in the car that sped away from the scene, a bullet from his leg with his own knife." He fled briefly to Syria and then to Egypt, where he resided for three years. According to the owner of a Cairo restaurant that Saddam frequented, "He was really quite lonely. He didn't have any friends. . . . I couldn't believe that such a bully who was picking fights all the time could grow up to be president of Iraq." Eventually Saddam returned home to marry his uncle's daughter, and was put in charge of a Baath Party farmers' organization. Then, after a coup briefly brought the Baathists to power in 1963 and another coup just as quickly dislodged them, Saddam wound up back behind bars. Rather than calm his revolutionary zeal, the time Saddam spent in captivity only seems to have fueled it, and he even converted prison guards to his murky cause. Two years later, Saddam escaped from jail. Returning to the Baath underground, he joined a party security force, the Jehaz Haneen, an Iraqi equivalent of Hitler's Brown Shirts. Saddam, who later became a devoted fan of *The Godfather,* would visit Baath opponents and slaughter them along with their families like a Mafia hit man, then dump their corpses in the street. The brutality reached a new pitch when the Baathists seized power again in 1968, and Saddam was installed as second-in-command and the real power behind his cousin General Ahmed Hassan Bakr. The tactics employed by Saddam and the Jehaz Haneen now became official policy.

As often is the case with Third World coups, a bloodbath accompanied Iraq's 1968 revolt. But this bloodbath never ended. Changing in name only, Saddam's Jehaz Haneen became the Mukhabarat, the intelligence and security force that terrorizes Iraq to this day. It began its work immediately. Only three months after coming to power, the new regime declared that it had uncovered a Zionist spy ring. Fourteen of these "spies," eleven of them Iraqi Jews, were promptly strung up before a crowd of thousands in a Baghdad square. "We hanged spies," Baghdad radio explained, "but the Jews crucified Christ." Over the following months, the regime executed not only Jews and communists, but also hundreds of Muslims accused of being linked to the "Zionist" plot. The executions were televised and the dead hung from lampposts.

As the new regime consolidated its grisly hold on power, so did Saddam. Not unlike Stalin, whose ruthlessness he admires and whose methods of rule he has carefully studied, Hussein proceeded to denounce and murder longtime colleagues on both the left and the right. Years of struggle, note Judith Miller and Laurie Mylroie, authors of *Saddam Hussein and the Crisis in the Gulf,* "made him far more ruthless in his determination to hold on to power and to break all who stood in his way or who might one day challenge his rule." Using Iraq's security services as a base, party vice chairman Saddam removed Bakr's other possible successors one by one. In *Iraq Since 1958,* Peter Sluglett and Marion-Farouk Sluglett detail how the aspiring dictator eliminated his fellow members of the Revolutionary Command Council at a July 1979 meeting. One of them, Muhyi Abd Husayn Mashadi, was tortured at Saddam's order, forced to recite a confession, and then made to stand in front of a Baath Party congress and implicate his fellow "plotters." As their names were mentioned, they were marched out of the hall to be shot—with their mouths taped shut lest they blurt out embarrassing last words, while Saddam sat watching silently, a cigar in his mouth. In case others missed the point, Saddam had the confessions videotaped and dispatched copies to Baath Party offices throughout the country.

That summer, Saddam shoved aside his kinsman, General Bakr, and by the end of the year he controlled all the levers of Iraqi power. Gone was any pretense of decentralized rule. Gone, too, was the ideological substance of Baathism. In its place arose a cult of personality, which, in its pervasive glorification of a single man, would soon rival even those built up around Stalin and Mao. ("To visit Iraq," observe Miller and Mylroie, "is to enter the land of Big Brother.") A towering portrait of Saddam hangs above nearly every village entrance, school, building and store. The ubiquitous portraits of Saddam the peasant, the soldier, the horseman; the wristwatches adorned with his mustachioed face; the claim to be descended from Nebuchadnezzar; the nineteen-volume official biography—these accoutrements of totalitarianism may seem today like parody. In Iraq, however, they reflect reality. The "Great Uncle," as Saddam likes his people to call him, has established one of the world's premier terror states.

"The Baath have saddled Iraq with two kinds of tyranny," writes Kanan Makiya in *Republic of Fear,* "the despot and his means of violence on the one hand, and his bureaucracy on the other." As to the first of these, Saddam rules his closest aides with the same brand of terror that he applies to Iraq's populace. Whether by ordering his ministers to go on the "Saddam Diet," treating them to frightening weapons demonstrations at company picnics, demanding that their foreign-language typewriters be registered to identify possible dissenters, or simply executing officials and their families as examples to the rest, "his excellency, the victorious, the glorious Saddam Hussein" commands a peculiar type of loyalty. And these are the privileged few. As one Iraqi told the *New York Times* in 1994, "Today I'd say not more than one million Iraqis are living in any real sense of the word. They are those who uphold Saddam's rule and those who protect him. They are given food and plenty of money."

In fact, when the ranks of the armed forces, police, security services and intelligence agencies are combined, the number of Iraqis bearing arms for Saddam Hussein well exceeds one million. Overlapping security organizations like the Military Intelligence Department, the Presidential Affairs Department, Party Security and State Internal Security spy on their own members, on one another and, of course, on average Iraqi citizens. "We are now in our Stalinist era," Saddam announced proudly in 1989. "We shall strike with an iron fist against the slightest deviation or backsliding." Even Saddam's military is suspect. During much of the Iran-Iraq war, Saddam kept his air force grounded for fear of a coup; he cancelled Armed Forces Day parades for the same reason; and he regularly executed senior officers for disloyalty or battlefield setbacks. As the Pentagon's Lieutenant General Thomas Kelly put it during the Gulf War, Saddam "has a fairly vigorous zero defects program." Indeed, the Baath Party investigates all officers, and three different security services are charged with rooting out dissenters in the army. And just in case his security services prove incapable of keeping the army away from the palace gates, Saddam employs a Baath Party militia armed with anti-tank weapons for the same purpose.

Iraq's guns, however, have mostly been reserved for use on its citizens. "Saddam Hussein exists in every corner, every place, every eyebrow and every heart in Iraq," the dictator (who habitually refers to himself in the third person) declared in 1982. Networks of informers

pervade the country, turning in those—including their own relatives—who make jokes at Saddam's expense or otherwise engage in
what passes for dissent in Iraqi society. Publicly insulting Saddam is
punishable by death. Britain's Index on Censorship reports a case
where a Baath Party member was arrested for being present at a gath-
ering where jokes were made about Hussein. For the crime of "not
informing the authorities" about the jokes, the party member and all
the males in his family were executed and the family's home was bulldozed. In another case documented by Amnesty International, a man's
tongue was sliced off for slandering the Iraqi dictator and then the
man was "driven around after the punishment while information
about his alleged offence was broadcast through a loudspeaker."

Instances of citizens disappearing are also routine. Human Rights
Watch reported in 1998 that Iraq had more unresolved "disappearances" than any other United Nations member state—over sixteen
thousand, according to the U.N. special rapporteur. Arbitrary and
deadly edicts issue from Saddam's palaces on a regular basis. In 1992,
the Iraqi leader gave new meaning to the phrase "command economy" when he arrested over five hundred of Baghdad's most prominent merchants on charges of "profiteering." Forty-two were executed
and their corpses strung up in front of their stores with placards that
labeled them as "Greedy Merchants." Two years later, the government
issued a decree stating that anyone who stole an item worth more
than $12 would have a hand amputated and, if a repeat offender,
would be branded. The constant flow of edicts and regulations
addresses mundane matters as well. Everything from street names
and university admissions to work regulations and building permits
comes directly from the presidential palace.

Mostly, though, Saddam simply relies on terror to keep his subjects in check. Marrying twenty-first-century technology to medieval
ruthlessness, his security apparatus has over the years fine-tuned the
art of torture and dismemberment. Although Saddam's lieutenants
all have the same general objective—rooting out dissent—they tai-
lor their tortures to their victims. For women, who are often tortured
to elicit confession from their male relatives, the security services
favor sexual assault and humiliation. According to Omar Ismael, a
captain in the Mukhabarat who fled Iraq in 2000, security agents

regularly drug the female relatives of government or military officials and film them being raped. The tapes are then used to blackmail or extract confessions from the officials. In one instance, Ismael was ordered to investigate Taha Abbas Hababi, the director of one of Iraq's intelligence agencies. "We found nothing against him after two months, so we made a tape of his daughter having sex with a man," recounts Ismael. "We had to drug her first." Soon after being sent the tape, Hababi was murdered anyway. According to Amnesty International, female prisoners are "hung upside down from the feet during menstruation. Objects have also been inserted into the vaginas of young women, causing the hymen to break." Amnesty International reports that when the security services torture women, interrogators routinely force the women's children to stay in the room and watch their mothers being debased.

Even the taboo against torturing children is routinely broken by Saddam's regime. Like many of the women the security services maltreat, children are tortured to elicit confessions from their families. Reports from defectors and human rights organizations detail a catalogue of atrocities committed against the young. Amnesty International explains, "Allegations received have included the following: the extraction of fingernails, beatings, whipping, sexual abuse, electrical shock treatment, and deprivation of food and of the use of toilet facilities." Another human rights group, Middle East Watch, records the testimony of a former detainee: "Each hour, security men opened the door and chose 3 to 5 of the prisoners—children or men—and removed them for torture. Later, their tortured bodies were thrown back into the cell. They were often bleeding and carried obvious signs of whipping and electric shocks. . . . At midnight, the security men took another three of the children, but because they were so savagely treated they were taken from the cell to a military hospital." It was later reported that twenty-nine of the children mentioned in this report were executed, their bodies returned to their families with their eyes gouged out. As for his own children, according to journalist Mark Bowden, Saddam's own son Uday has boasted that he and his brother Qusay were taken by their father to Iraqi prisons to watch torture and executions as part of a "toughening up" process.

While the regime visits unspeakable punishment upon the wives and children of suspected dissidents, it reserves the worst fate for the accused themselves. In recent years, several reports of mass executions of adult males have leaked out of Iraq. One of these concerns a mass killing that occurred in 1998 at Abu Ghraib prison, an Iraqi jail that holds thousands of inmates accused of "anti-government activities." In interviews with Radio Free Iraq and the *London Observer,* whose substance has been corroborated by Western diplomats, a senior Mukhabarat officer who served on the prison's supervisory committee testified that on a single day in April 1998, his committee executed two thousand dissidents: "Some were hanged. Others were shot. Each victim was shot once in the head." The executions have gone on for years. According to Human Rights Watch, "Each year there have been reports of dozens—sometimes hundreds—of deaths, with bodies of victims at times left in the street or returned to families bearing marks of torture: eyes gouged out, fingernails missing, genitals cut off, and terrible wounds and burns." Here, for instance, is testimony from a mother who was called to the morgue in 1982 to retrieve the body of a son who had been held without charge: "I looked around and saw 9 bodies stretched out on the floor with him. Another's body carried the marks of a hot domestic iron. Another had his legs axed. One of them looked hanged."

If Saddam is capable of sinister cruelty toward everyday Iraqis, his treatment of Iraq's ethnic and religious groups—particularly the Kurds and Shiites—is virtually genocidal. When, in 1980, Saddam's forces invaded Iran, most of whose citizens are Shiites, their coreligionists in Iraq immediately became suspect. Accordingly, Saddam began to empty Iraq's cities of their own Shiite populations. He also embarked on a program of deportation, expelling some thirty-five thousand Shiites from Iraq by the summer of 1980. That summer, too, the Mukhabarat arrested Iraq's leading Shiite cleric, Mohammad Baqr al-Sadr. It then murdered him by setting his beard on fire and hammering nails into his head. As Iraq's eight-year war with Iran ground on, the plight of the Shiites worsened. By war's end in 1988, Saddam's regime had tortured, expelled or murdered tens of thousands of innocent Iraqis for no reason other than their religious affiliation. And worse was to come.

Three years later, during the closing days of Operation Desert Storm, the Shiites of southern Iraq took a cue from the first President Bush and rose up against Saddam's rule. "By March 7, a little over a week after the rebellion had exploded," Sandra Mackey recounts in *The Reckoning*, "Basra, Najaf, and Karbala as well as other Shia towns in the south were prime to become killing fields." As the American military stood on the sidelines, Saddam dispatched his special forces to crush the revolt. His troops fanned out across southern Iraq, threatening to kill every Shiite, hanging clerics, looting religious shrines and bulldozing Shiite graveyards. While the Iraqi media branded the Shiites part of "a dirty, foreign conspiracy," the Iraqi army pillaged, raped and murdered its way through town after town, killing thousands in the space of a few months. Many of the survivors fled east to Iran. Others fled to the countryside and nearby marshes, where, it was hoped, simple geography would constrain Baghdad's reach. Saddam, however, soon transformed the waterways, islands and reed beds of southern Iraq into an arid death pit.

Until the 1991 uprising, the southern marsh area of Iraq had been home to hundreds of thousands of Shiites (known as marsh Arabs) who lived in the surrounding towns and in the marshes themselves. A videotape obtained by the U.N. shows several Iraqi army generals being instructed in 1991 to "wipe out" the local populations. The U.S. State Department later obtained an Iraqi army document, captured by anti-Saddam forces, that instructed Iraqi forces in the area to "withdraw all foodstuffs, ban the sale of fish, poison the water and burn the villages." The same year, full-scale military assaults on marsh villages ensued, including "indiscriminate bombardments on civilian settlements," according to a 1992 U.N. report. In the villages of Adil, al-Salaam, Mainona and al-Majar, residents were confined to their houses and then subjected to artillery attacks. David Rose reports that Saddam's forces may have murdered as many as 100,000 Shiites during the campaign. "They brought them in buses, and they left in lorries, dripping with blood," a senior Iraqi defector told Rose. "Every lorry we and the special security agency possess was being used for dead bodies, taking them to mass graves. We kept each grave open for days; when it was full, we'd dig another one." Baghdad "held the marsh area subject to an internal economic blockade," said a U.N.

report, while also "restricting the inflow of basic foodstuffs and medicaments needed by the inhabitants." Then it cut off the water.

While most governments drain swamps to build and populate, Baghdad drains them for a very different reason. Ostensibly in the name of creating a central waterway to irrigate the salted flats of the area, Saddam ordered the construction of massive dikes to channel the water of the Tigris and the Euphrates away from the marshes. As a result, much of the marshland has been transformed into a parched desert. When Shiite families abandoned their homes, Iraqi army units moved in. The U.N. called the program "a method to facilitate government control over the population in the area." But human rights organizations made clear the program's true purpose when they reported that agents of the Mukhabarat dumped poison into the now-diminished streams that wind through the marshes—sickening villagers and killing fish, turtles and other marsh life.

Iraq's Shiites, like the Sunni regime that persecutes them, are mostly Arabs. That probably accounts for why their fate, however cruel, pales beside the plight of Iraq's Kurds, who enjoy no such ethnic kinship. Dispersed between Turkey, Iran, Iraq and Syria, the Kurds constitute a distinct ethnic group—non-Arab, stateless, and persecuted by their host countries for centuries. No regime has treated them more savagely than Saddam's. Most Iraqi Kurds live in the north of Iraq, and it is there that some of the most horrendous crimes of the last part of the twentieth century were committed. The Kurdish struggle for autonomy from Iraq long predates Saddam Hussein's arrival in Baghdad. But when Saddam seized power, the tactics used to quell the struggle immediately became more violent—acquiring "the character of a racist war of extermination," as the Kurdish Democratic Party put it. Not a year after the coup that brought Hussein to power, the atrocities began. In 1969, the U.N. reported that Iraqi agents in the Kurdish province of Mosul burned almost seventy women and children alive in a cave. Soon the Baath regime had launched a campaign of ethnic cleansing, deporting forty thousand Kurds in 1971 and relocating Arab settlers in their place. Such was Saddam's obsession with the Kurds that during the October 1973 attack against Israel—which Iraq joined—he kept the bulk of Iraq's military establishment in reserve, choosing to fight the Kurds instead of the Jews.

The following year, the Iraqi military, equipped with helicopters, tanks and napalm-carrying jets, shelled Kurdish towns, massacred one thousand surrendering Kurdish fighters, deported the residents of entire villages to the desert and, according to *The Times* of London, left half of Iraq's Kurdish population homeless. In one notorious incident during the 1974 offensive, Iraqi bombers decimated a column of 250,000 Kurds desperately fleeing toward Iran. In another, the army burned two major Kurdish towns, Zakho and Qala'at Diza, to the ground. Amidst the deathscape that Saddam created, mass arrests, public hangings and summary executions became common events. The only glimmer of hope the Kurds had came from Washington. At the time, the United States, then allied with the shah of Iran, was supplying them with arms to fight the Iraqi army. But in 1975, after Henry Kissinger brokered an accord between Baghdad and the shah, the United States cut off the flow of arms to the Kurds, and their resistance collapsed.

With the Kurds subdued, Saddam's gaze shifted in the late 1970s toward Iran, where eight years of trench warfare would soon ravage his army. Yet the Iran-Iraq War hardly gained the Kurds a reprieve. On the contrary, Baghdad charged that the Kurds, like the Shiites, had aided the Iranian war effort. For this sin, the Kurds earned the distinction of being the first ethnic group since the Holocaust to be gassed by their own government. In a tape obtained by Human Rights Watch, Ali Hassan al-Majid, who directed the murderous effort, boasted to his fellow members of the Iraqi regime: "I will kill them all with chemical weapons! Who is going to say anything? The international community? Fuck them!" He was right. While the international community turned a blind eye, the Iraqi air force dropped chemical weapons on the Iraqi towns of Halabja, Goktapa and as many as two hundred other villages. Human Rights Watch estimates that the assaults of the late 1980s claimed the lives of about 100,000 Kurds. The Kurds themselves put the figure closer to 200,000. Whatever the number, this much is evident: Saddam's "Al-Anfal" campaign reached near-genocidal proportions. "Most of the Kurds who were murdered in the Anfal were not killed by poison gas," Jeffrey Goldberg has written in the *New Yorker*, "rather the genocide was carried out, in large part, in the traditional manner, with roundups at night, mass executions, and anonymous burials." Those not murdered instantly either fled across the same routes they had traveled a decade before, were expelled from Kurdish lands, or were herded into filthy camps where they soon starved.

Nor have the survivors fared well in the years since. Having encouraged the Kurds, along with the Shiites, to rise up against Saddam Hussein during the 1991 Gulf War, the first President Bush abandoned them to their fate as soon as the United States ejected Iraqi forces from Kuwait. For the third time in two decades, Saddam slaughtered Kurds by the thousands, while survivors fled north over the mountains and into Turkey. This time, televised images of refugee columns proved too much to bear, and following a massive American relief effort, the United States announced that northern Iraq would henceforth be a "no-fly" zone—that is, Iraqi warplanes would no longer be allowed to patrol and terrorize Kurdish Iraq. This allowed the Kurds to establish a safe haven under an American umbrella. Then history repeated itself.

In the late summer of 1996, the Iraqi army struck north toward the Kurdish city of Irbil. Other than directing a fusillade of cruise missiles at targets south of Baghdad, the Clinton administration did nothing. CIA officers and other U.S. officials working with Kurdish leaders were pulled out of the region, and hundreds of their Kurdish colleagues were promptly executed. Today, the Iraqi army routinely mounts attacks on Kurdish villages in northern Iraq, evicting families from their homes, forcing Kurds to officially renounce their nationality, and relocating Arab families in their place.

TWO

Aggression Abroad

Saddam Hussein is a brutal dictator. But do his crimes against his own people justify taking up arms against him? There are some who claim that no matter how horrific a government's treatment of its citizens, outside powers have no legal basis for intervening in the affairs of a sovereign nation. Even today, even after the Holocaust, Pol Pot and Rwanda, many devotees of *realpolitik* believe that a government, whether or not it is "legitimate" by Western standards, should be able to do as it pleases within its borders. Former House Republican majority leader Dick Armey supports such a position, arguing that we should "let [Saddam Hussein] bluster, let him rant and rave all he wants and let that be a matter between him and his own country. As long as he behaves himself within his own borders, we should not be addressing any attack or resources against him."

So, for a moment, let us pretend that Iraq is the Netherlands of the Arab world: Its citizens enjoy unprecedented rights, speak their minds and elect their leaders. There are no massacres, no deportations, no disappearances or late-night knocks on the door. Even if all this were true, Saddam Hussein's regime would still qualify as one of the world's most dangerous, and one that requires dealing with—not because of what it does at home, but because of what it does abroad.

In international law, the corollary to the principle of national sovereignty is the prohibition against aggression—the use of force by one country against another, unless justified by self-defense. Article 2(4) of the U.N. Charter forbids "the threat or use of force against the territorial integrity or political independence of any state." Saddam himself routinely appeals to the Charter, complaining to the

15

U.N. about American and Iranian "aggression." (Iraq is also a party to, among other international agreements, the Geneva Protocol forbidding the use of chemical weapons and the 1948 Genocide Convention.) In fact, the Charter's proscription against interstate aggression has largely been observed: While there have been dozens of civil wars since World War II, during the same period there have been a relatively small number of wars between states. As it happens, Saddam is responsible for quite a few of them. During the two decades of his rule, Iraq has committed acts of aggression against Iran, Kuwait and Israel. "Pyramids of skulls," in the words of Jordan's King Hussein, are what they produced.

Only months after seizing power in 1979, Saddam ordered Iraqi forces to invade Iran. "I'm going to march into Teheran and pull the beard off of Khomeini's face," the Iraqi dictator boasted to Saudi Arabia's King Fahd. The conflict that followed ranked as one of the longest and bloodiest conventional wars of the twentieth century. The Iran-Iraq War lasted eight years, claiming the lives of at least a million people and maiming twice that number. And when it was all over, Saddam had accomplished exactly nothing. Despite billions of dollars spent in eight years of bloodletting, the battle lines separating the two armies had barely budged.

The minimal aim of the war, Saddam declared at its outset, was to regain the Shatt al Arab waterway that Iraq had surrendered to Iran in 1975. So five days before invading Iraq, Saddam announced that the 1975 treaty was no longer valid, and for good measure, he tore it up in front of the television cameras. Saddam's broader aim, which he spelled out in several speeches that same year, was to bring about the collapse of Iran's theocratic regime. The decision to invade Iran, wrote Michael Sterner in *Foreign Affairs* while the war still raged, "must be ranked as one of this century's worst strategic miscalculations."

Exactly how badly Saddam had miscalculated became apparent within weeks. At first, the Iraqi army pushed deep into Iranian territory, taking Teheran's clerics by surprise and achieving several battlefield victories. Indeed, Saddam believed the war would be over within a month. But he soon confronted unexpected resistance. Iranian commanders enjoyed a three-to-one manpower advantage over the Iraqi army and began employing those numbers to devastating effect, using "human waves" to overrun Iraqi positions. As a result, Iraq's forces quickly bogged down, and in 1981 Iran launched a series of successful offensives, which ejected Saddam's forces from Iranian territory. The following year brought more victories for Iran, filling its prison camps with tens of thousands of captured Iraqi soldiers. At one point during 1982, Saddam himself was almost captured. "While driving around the rear of the fighting," write Miller and Mylroie, "Saddam's convoy was besieged by Iranian troops. The only Iraqi force close enough to relieve Saddam was commanded by General Maher Abdul Rashid, a Tikriti general who was not on speaking terms with him." Rashid refused to relieve the cornered dictator until Saddam pleaded for help in the name of Rashid's uncle, whom he had murdered several years earlier.

By June 1982 his forces were faring so poorly on the battlefield that Saddam declared a unilateral ceasefire, proposing instead that Iraq and Iran align themselves against Israel. The Iranians responded by advancing into Iraq itself.

Needless to say, Iran's battlefield successes had little to do with the tactical genius of its commanders, who relied on raw recruits anxious for paradise to clear minefields with their bodies. Rather, as one strategist observed at the time, the "primary reason Iran was not defeated at the outset of the war lay in the inept strategy and tactics of the Iraqis." And those tactics came directly from Baghdad. Throughout the war, Saddam routinely traveled to the front to direct battles himself.

In fact, Saddam bears responsibility not only for Iraq's unlawful invasion of Iran, but also for the lawless and inhumane tactics that it employed during the fighting. Those tactics make up an encyclopedia of Geneva Convention violations. To begin with, Saddam had no reservations about waging war on Iran's civilian population. As part of his "War of the Cities," Saddam ordered his forces to launch missile attacks on Iranian towns, mosques and schools. During the eight-year war, countless Iranian neighborhoods were wiped out by Iraqi rocket attacks. According to U.S. intelligence reports, during three months in 1988 alone, Iraq launched at least 189 Scud missiles at Teheran. As for the tactics Saddam directed against Iranian soldiers, a favorite was electrocution. ("We are frying them like eggplants," an

Iraqi officer boasted.) *Los Angeles Times* reporter Mark Fineman described a 1984 battle where the Iraqi army "fried" the enemy: "Iraqi gun batteries fired just enough artillery to force the Revolutionary Guards from their marsh boats, and, when hundreds of them had been forced to continue their advance through the lagoons on foot, the men manning the Iraqi generators flipped a few switches and sent thousands of volts of electricity surging through the marshland. Within seconds, hundreds of Iranians were electrocuted."

Saddam's army also captured and imprisoned tens of thousands of Iranian soldiers. The brutal treatment of the Iranians, which gained the West's attention after reports filtered out of Iraqi prison camps in the mid-1980s, spurred several U.N. inquiries. In 1985, a team commissioned by the U.N. secretary general to investigate the camps reported, "the allegations most frequently heard related to blows on the head and other beatings with batons, truncheons, or wire cables." Prisoners "spoke of being suspended upside down from ceilings or ventilators, or having the soles of their feet whipped or beaten, or electric shocks administered to various parts of their bodies, including their genital organs, of burnings with cigarettes, and in some cases, mock executions." In 1990, two years after the Iran-Iraq War had ended, Iraq was still holding as many as fourteen thousand Iranian prisoners. Even then, Andrew Whitley of Middle East Watch testified before the House Foreign Affairs Committee that prisoners were being "systematically tortured to extract information, gain cooperation, mute opposition or to set an example to discourage others." As late as 2002, Iraq was still holding up to three thousand Iranian captives in custody.

And, of course, Saddam gassed Iranian soldiers and civilians. Between 1984 and 1988, six separate teams of U.N. investigators documented instances of Iraq using chemical weapons on Iranians. In 1988, Iraq's foreign minister, Tariq Aziz, openly admitted that poison gas was enshrined in official Iraqi war policy. The same year, the Security Council released a report that blamed Iraq for using mustard gas in attacks against Iranian cities. It also voted unanimously to condemn Iraq for its "more intense and frequent" use of chemical weapons in violation of the Geneva Protocols. Baghdad escaped harsher censure only because its foe was also a pariah state whose suffering evoked little sympathy in Western capitals. But none of this made the Iranians' suffering any less real. Beginning in 1984, Iraq bombarded Iran with chemical weapons for five consecutive years, killing and injuring thousands and sending gassing victims to Western Europe's hospitals for the first time since World War I. A U.N. report details how an Iraqi infantry assault was preceded by a two-hour artillery barrage with nerve gas and cyanide shells. "The first symptoms consisted of a burning in the eyes and various parts of the body," the report stated. Then the skin of victims turned violet and blisters and lesions formed, and eventually the skin turned black. Heavily exposed victims experienced lung and kidney failure, blindness and, for the unlucky remainder, death. "If you gave me a pesticide to throw at these swarms of insects to make them breathe it and die," an Iraqi general told the *Washington Post* in 1984, "I'd use it." In all likelihood, he already had.

Even though the war against Iran was a catastrophic failure by any objective standard, its conclusion left Saddam giddy with feelings of invulnerability. Two years after the last shot was fired, he sent his forces rolling south toward Kuwait. As Iraq's army dug in along the Kuwaiti border in late July 1990, world leaders, including American officials, refused to acknowledge the obvious. Among the reasons offered for Baghdad's "saber-rattling" was that Saddam meant to pressure OPEC into raising oil prices; that he sought to erase $2 billion in debt owed to Kuwait; that he wanted to lease tiny Kuwaiti islands in the Gulf; and that he wished to persuade the Kuwaitis to reach an accommodation over a disputed oilfield along the border. In the days leading up to the war, progress was made on all of these issues. Yet, on August 2, Saddam invaded anyway. With the aid of several armored divisions, amphibious landings and helicopters ferrying special forces into Kuwait City, hundreds of thousands of Iraqi troops poured across the border. In a matter of hours, the country was theirs.

There were no mitigating issues, no diplomatic gray areas. Rarely has the responsibility for a conflict fallen so clearly on one side, and the international community promptly returned a unanimous verdict. On the very day of the invasion, the U.N. Security Council approved a resolution condemning the aggression and demanding "that Iraq withdraw immediately and unconditionally." Over the following days, the Security Council would vote unanimously to ban trade with Iraq; Arab leaders would agree to dispatch a pan-Arab force to defend Saudi Arabia; and the United States and the Soviet Union would demand that Iraqi forces quit Kuwait. Finally, on November 29, the Security Council authorized the use of force to eject Saddam's army. None of this, however, seemed to make the slightest impression on Saddam. On the contrary, he declared Kuwait to be Iraq's nineteenth province and ignored a daily stream of offers to mediate his dispute with the Kuwaitis—offers that would have allowed him to save face. Instead, he railed publicly about the "mother of all battles if the West sought to intervene," all the while assuring fellow Arab leaders that it would never come to that. "My brother," Saddam told Saudi Arabia's King Fahd, "don't worry about this. It's not a big deal." When others warned Saddam that he risked the wrath of the United States, he became downright delusional. "I was barking at the moon," Egyptian president Hosni Mubarak recounted. "This man is crazy," echoed Syrian president Hafez al-Assad. "He thinks because he fought the Iranians he can threaten the Israelis and the Americans. He doesn't know what real military power is."

As with the Iran-Iraq War before it, Saddam's conduct of the Gulf War was brutal, ignoring any distinction between soldiers and civilians. He dispatched 7,000 Mukhabarat agents to Kuwait City. Along with 430,000 regular troops in the country, they proceeded to ransack the capital, establish interrogation and torture centers, and execute Kuwaitis in the streets. (A 1992 U.S. government report estimates that Saddam's forces executed or tortured to death over 1,000 Kuwaitis during the occupation.) At the same time, Saddam's agents conducted vast sweeps throughout the city, in which thousands of civilians were rounded up, imprisoned and carted off to Iraq. A State Department report published in 1993 found Iraqi forces in Kuwait responsible for the following crimes against Kuwaiti civilians: "Electric shock was applied to sensitive parts of the body (nose, mouth, genitalia); electric drills were used to penetrate chests, legs, or arms. Victims were beaten until bones were broken, skulls were crushed and faces disfigured. Some victims were killed in acid baths. One hundred fifty-three children between the ages of 1 and 13 were killed for various reasons and 57 mentally ill individuals killed simply because of their handicap." Such was the horror of this particular report that the first Bush administration had refused to release it, fearing that it would call into question the administration's failure to oust Saddam after Desert Storm.

As with the Iranians before them, hundreds of Kuwaiti POWs disappeared into thin air. U.N. Resolution 686, passed on March 2, 1991, as part of the Gulf War ceasefire agreed to by Saddam, stipulated that Iraq "arrange for immediate access to and release of all prisoners of war under the auspices of the International Committee of the Red Cross." Yet in February 1993, the Kuwaiti government submitted records to the ICRC—many of them gleaned from captured Iraqi documents detailing the arrest and transfer of Kuwaiti prisoners—showing that 605 of the POWs taken by Iraq were still unaccounted for. Two-thirds were civilians kidnapped from their homes or picked up by Iraqi forces on the street. Seven were women, 24 were elderly, and 124 were students. Baghdad denies their existence to this day.

There were also Americans captured during the war. Their Iraqi captors routinely beat American POWs, spat on them, forced them to urinate on the American flag, examined their genitals to determine if any were Jewish, and subjected them to mock executions. And lest we forget Saddam's famous stab at public relations during the Gulf War—when he asked a Western child captive "Are you getting your milk and cornflakes too?"—the Iraqi dictator seized thousands of foreign hostages, including American civilians, to be used as "human shields."

Iraq's unlawful conduct during the war against Kuwait extended even to the environment. According to a report by the Environmental Protection Agency, Saddam Hussein systematically ignited or otherwise crippled 749 oil wells during Iraq's retreat from Kuwait in February 1991, causing 610 well blazes. By June, those fires were emitting roughly two million tons of carbon dioxide daily into the atmosphere. "Soot falls like gritty snowflakes, streaking windshields and staining clothes," *Time* magazine reported of the war's aftermath. "From the overcast skies drips a greasy black rain, while sheets of gooey oil slap against a polluted shore." Making things worse, Saddam ordered his forces to sabotage Kuwaiti oil production facilities, causing the discharge of nearly eight million barrels of oil into the Persian Gulf. The resulting sludge killed thousands of seabirds, turtles and other animals that inhabit the Gulf coastline. It also poisoned salt marshes, swamps, creeks and streams throughout the region. Recognizing the extent of the destruction, the U.N. Security Council held Iraq directly responsible. Security Council Resolution 687 of April 3, 1991, stipulates "that Iraq is liable under international law for any direct loss, damage, including environmental damage and the depletion of natural resources as a result of Iraq's unlawful invasion and occupation of Kuwait." Needless to say, Saddam has not paid damages, and the Gulf's ecosystem has yet to recover.

Kuwait was not the only nation to be attacked by Saddam during the Gulf War. The Iraqi dictator also lobbed missiles at Saudi Arabia, Bahrain and Israel. In fact, the Jewish state absorbed no less than thirty-nine Iraqi Scuds. Israel was not even a member of the alliance arrayed against Baghdad—having been persuaded by the Bush administration that its participation would doom the Arab coalition. Nor, for the same reason, did it retaliate against the missile attacks. Still, the bombardment it endured was no mystery. Even though it does not share a border with Israel, Iraq has participated in all of the Arab-Israeli wars. As other Arab regimes do, Saddam uses Israel to divert attention from his own failings at home. But the ideology on which Saddam's rule is based, Baathism, also includes a commitment to the "liberation" of Palestine. It deems the Arab-Israeli conflict "a life and death struggle" and "a question of to be or not to be." As for Saddam, he routinely inveighs against "foul Jewish usurpers" and likens Israel to "a cancerous tumor that should be excised from Palestine."

Unlike some of his fellow Arab leaders, Saddam really means it. With the help of the French, he began construction on a nuclear power plant shortly after his rise to power. Its purpose was clear: foreign countries "should assist the Arabs to obtain . . . the nuclear bomb in order to confront Israel's existing bombs," Saddam declared in 1981. When the Israeli air force laid waste to the Osirak nuclear plant that same year, the Iraqi dictator only stepped up his threats to destroy the Jewish state. "By God," he vowed in a 1990 speech threatening to use chemical weapons against Israel, "we will make the fire eat up half of Israel if it tries to do anything against Iraq." Israel never did try. Nonetheless, Saddam launched missiles at the Jewish state during the Gulf War, hoping to bring Israel into the conflict and thereby rupture the U.S.-Arab coalition. A disaster was barely averted when, according to U.N. weapons inspector Richard Butler, Iraq fired a missile at Israel's Dimona nuclear power plant. It missed.

The Gulf War ended on February 27, 1991, but Saddam's battle against Israel continues to this day. In the years since Desert Storm, Iraqi officials have stated explicitly that Iraq maintains biological weapons for use against Israel. Saddam's son Uday boasts that Baghdad possesses "weapons of comprehensive destruction" for this purpose and that "the extinction of the Zionist entity was a necessity dictated both by the will of God, and the need to recover exclusive Arab rights in Palestine." Saddam has kept up a steady stream of invective, too. Nor did the Arab-Israeli peace process of the 1990s make much of an impression in Baghdad, whose media occasionally urged that the "traitor" Arafat be dealt with just as Egyptian president Anwar Sadat was—through assassination.

The most recent tactic Saddam has employed against the peace process involves subsidizing the families of Palestinian suicide bombers. On Saddam's gruesome pay scale, the families of gunmen who die in attacks on Israelis receive $10,000, while relatives of suicide bombers earn $25,000. Exactly which suicide bombers qualify for Saddam's bounty has become a source of disagreement. Iraq stipulates that only those who blow themselves up with explosive belts receive full payment. According to London's *Daily Telegraph,* "This has angered the parents of six young men from Jenin who went to the nearby town of Afula with a gun and opened fire, only to be shot dead themselves. They merited only the reward for an ordinary martyr."

Israel is not the only country against which the Iraqi dictator wields this peculiar brand of aggression. The United States also has been affected by Iraqi-sponsored acts of terror. Contrary to the claims of skeptics, evidence of a link between Saddam and Al Qaeda is not limited to ambiguous accounts of meetings between their emissaries said to have taken place in the Czech Republic prior to September 11. American officials have recently documented contacts between Iraqi and Al Qaeda agents, as well as "solid evidence of the presence in Iraq of Al Qaeda members, including some that have been in Baghdad," according to CIA director George Tenet. For the past three years, a band of Islamic radicals called Ansar al-Islam, led by a suspected Iraqi intelligence operative, have waged a terror campaign against Kurdish officials. According to a report in *Time,* the group was trained by Al Qaeda forces in Afghanistan and returned to Iraq after the battle of Tora Bora. As a result, U.S. officials now believe there are hundreds of Al Qaeda cadres operating in Iraq. It is not plausible that Saddam remains blind to their presence. "In a vicious, repressive dictatorship that exercises near-total control over its population," Defense Secretary Donald Rumsfeld pointed out last August, "it's very hard to imagine that the government is not aware of what's taking place in the country."

Indeed, Iraq's ambassador to Turkey and a close Saddam ally, Farouk Hijazi, traveled in 1998 to Kandahar, Afghanistan, where he is reported to have met with Osama bin Laden and invited him to seek refuge in Iraq. Before that, when bin Laden was living in Sudan, Saddam was channeling funds to him and the radical Islamic regime that ruled the country. "We were convinced that money from Iraq was going to bin Laden, who was then sending it to places they wanted it to go," said Stanley Bedlington, a senior CIA analyst who monitored bin Laden in Sudan. In 1994, according to a report in *USA Today,* the CIA obtained intelligence that one of those places was Algeria, where Iraq was using bin Laden to funnel money to Islamic terrorists who sought to overthrow that country's government. And in October 2002, George Tenet declared, based on credible reports, that "Iraq has provided training to Al Qaeda members in the areas of poisons and gases and making conventional bombs."

While we may never know the full extent of the murky ties between Saddam and bin Laden, we do know that Saddam is a terrorist. It was Saddam's operatives, not bin Laden's, who attempted to assassinate former President Bush in 1993. On April 14 of that year, two Iraqi nationals, Raad al-Asadi and Wali al-Ghazali, plotted to kill Bush while he was visiting Kuwait. The Kuwaitis captured the two before they could carry out their plan and handed them over to the FBI. Under interrogation, they admitted that Iraqi intelligence agents had supplied them with a car bomb to kill the president. Indeed, the evidence proved credible enough to persuade the Clinton administration to retaliate with a missile attack against an Iraqi intelligence facility. It was during 1993 as well that the first attempt to destroy the World Trade Center occurred. As it happens, the bombing's ringleader, Ramzi Yousef, arrived in New York bearing a phony Iraqi passport and an equally phony identity, which some investigators believe was forged by Iraqi agents in Kuwait during the 1990–91 occupation. Another World Trade Center suspect, Abdul Yasin, fled to Iraq after the bombing, where he is believed to be still hiding.

Perhaps the most convincing evidence of Iraq's involvement in terrorism is that it harbors well-known terrorists. The death in August of the notorious terrorist Abu Nidal in Baghdad provided a useful reminder that Iraq has become a state of last resort for the pariahs of the international terror community. As White House spokesman Ari Fleischer pointed out when news broke of the death, "The fact that only Iraq would give safe haven to Abu Nidal demonstrates the Iraqi regime's complicity with global terror." In addition to figures such as Abu Nidal, Saddam has extended his country's hospitality to an alphabet soup of terrorist organizations. According to the State Department's most recent terrorism report, last year "Iraq provided bases to several terrorist groups including the Mujahedin-e-Khalq (MEK), the Kurdistan Workers' Party (PKK), the Palestine Liberation Front (PLF), and the Abu Nidal organization (ANO)."

In 2001, the Popular Front for the Liberation of Palestine raised its profile in the West Bank and the Gaza Strip by carrying out successful terrorist attacks against Israeli targets. For this, the Iraqi regime rewarded the PFLP with a series of ostentatious receptions, including meetings with an Iraqi vice president and a deputy prime minister. Hamas, too, has benefited from Saddam's generosity, apparently receiving training in weapons and even suicide bombing at Iraq's Salman Pak terrorist camp.

That camp is a school for terrorists, offering classes in assassination, hijacking, kidnapping and sabotage. "We were training these people to attack installations important to the United States," a senior Iraqi defector told the *New York Times*. Salman Pak is best known to the Western media for the training it provides on an authentic Boeing 707, parked squarely in the middle of the camp. A parade of defectors have described how the plane is used to school terrorists—including Islamic extremists from across the Arab world—in the art of seizing commercial aircraft. "They are even trained how to use utensils for food, like forks, and knives provided in the plane," another defector told *Aviation Week and Space Technology.* "They are trained how to plant horror within the passengers by doing such actions." The stories about the camp and the 707 have been corroborated in recent years by, among others, Charles Duelfer, the former deputy executive chairman of U.N. weapons inspections in Iraq, who saw the plane on several occasions in exactly the location the defectors had described. Space Imaging, the commercial satellite firm, also photographed the plane on April 25, 2000, in the place specified by the defectors. With Saddam's record of aggression and terror, none of this should have come as a surprise.

THREE

Weapons of Mass Destruction

A dictator who murders his own countrymen may not be America's business. A dictator who threatens his neighbors may not be America's business. Even a dictator who sponsors terrorism may not be America's business. But a dictator who does all these things and not only possesses but uses weapons of mass destruction—surely that is America's business. "Predators of the twenty-first century," said Bill Clinton in a blunt 1998 warning, "will be all the more lethal if we allow them to build arsenals of nuclear, chemical and biological weapons and the missiles to deliver them. There is no more clear example of this threat than Saddam Hussein's Iraq."

Saddam has barely bothered to conceal the threat he poses. Indeed, flaunting his destructive powers seems to be an intrinsic aspect of his governance. Rarely before has a regime detailed its own illegal arsenal so meticulously; and thanks largely to UNSCOM, the U.N. weapons inspection program that was established to record and destroy Iraq's illegal arsenal in the aftermath of the Gulf War, rarely before have those details been so thoroughly documented and publicized. Iraq's efforts to acquire WMD long predate the Gulf War, as the ravaged Iranians and Kurds will attest. According to UNSCOM's final report, submitted to the Security Council in January 1999, Iraq began its effort to develop biological weapons in 1973 or 1974, when Saddam was still vice president. Iraq itself concedes that from 1974 to 1978 it conducted "research on micro-organisms for military purposes." In the mid-1970s, Iraq also began a campaign to develop and acquire chemical weapons. It constructed chemical factories, produced the raw materials required for the weapons, and purchased chemical ingredients from reliable suppliers like Germany and France.

France also helped Saddam construct a nuclear plant at Osirak. Fearing that this facility might someday be used to produce nuclear weapons that would be employed against them, the Israelis attacked it by air in 1981 and destroyed it. (For this they received condemnation from around the globe.) Saddam then resolved to diversify the weapons of mass destruction in his inventory. He went on a spending spree, purchasing tens of billions of dollars worth of military equipment from the Europeans, establishing front companies to produce weapons components, and accelerating Iraq's own research and production lines. During much of the 1980s, Iraq was the world's single largest purchaser of weapons. According to the U.N., it imported 819 long-range combat missiles and then modified more than half of them to reach even more distant targets. Through its "State Establishment for Pesticide Production," which happened to be headquartered at Salman Pak, the camp where terrorists trained, Iraq also acquired large amounts of biological agents. According to statements made to U.N. inspectors by General Nizar Attar, who presided over Iraq's biological research and development programs, Iraq drew up plans in 1986 to convert these agents into weapons. The deadly agents included anthrax, botulinum, brucellosis and tularaemia. According to the U.N., "field tests of BW [biological warfare] agents started in late 1987/early 1988," and by 1989, biological agents were used in "field testing aerial bombs, rockets and other munitions." Among other things, U.N. inspectors found that the regime had been employing these agents in "aerosol dissemination studies," spraying toxins on monkeys and other small animals. By the end of the decade, Iraq possessed some 200,000 "special munitions," of which some 100,000 had been filled with chemical or biological substances.

Meanwhile, on the nuclear front, UNSCOM discovered that Iraq had continued to amass bomb-making materials throughout the 1980s. According to David Kay, who led weapons inspections in Iraq immediately after the Gulf War, Baghdad launched an urgent effort to obtain nuclear weapons in the aftermath of the Osirak attack. By the time of the Gulf War, writes Kay, Iraq had acquired a considerable stock of enriched uranium, and "design, component testing, and the construction of manufacturing facilities for actual bomb production were well advanced." It was subsequently determined that over twenty thousand people were employed in Iraq's clandestine nuclear weapons program, an astonishing fact given that the very agency charged with monitoring Iraq's nuclear program, the International Atomic Energy Agency (IAEA), had no idea that this massive program even existed.

On April 18, 1991, as part of the Gulf War ceasefire agreement, Iraq delivered to UNSCOM details about the quantity and type of its missile and biological and chemical weapons programs. By its own admission, Iraq possessed nearly 10,000 nerve gas warheads, 1,500 chemical weapons, 412 tons of chemical weapon agents, 25 long-range missiles and numerous aircraft drop-tanks filled with biological agents, and much else besides. Yet during nearly a decade of U.N. weapons inspections, Iraq would routinely declare that it had only a fraction of the nuclear, biological or chemical material it was later revealed to possess. By the fall of 1991, for instance, weapons inspectors had found nearly ten times the number of chemical weapons that Baghdad had declared in its arsenal. The pattern of obfuscation and revision would repeat itself every time inspectors stumbled across a new cache. As one section in a typical UNSCOM report notes, "In the original declaration of the contents of the Al-Hussein missile warheads, in September 1995, no mention was made of aflatoxin. Later Iraq stated that two had been filled with aflatoxin. Finally this number was adjusted to four."

The bureaucratic understatement of the UNSCOM reports obscures the frustration and harassment that inspectors regularly endured in their search for the truth. Armed with U.N. Resolution 687, which allowed them "unconditional and unrestricted" access to every corner of Iraq's missile, chemical, biological and nuclear programs, the U.N.'s weapons inspectors arrived in Baghdad in June 1991. Almost immediately they ran into trouble. In September the Iraqis detained an inspection team outside a Baghdad nuclear facility, seizing their documents and holding the team's members for four days in a parking lot. That same year, chief weapons inspector David Kay reported that "significant documentary material and equipment" had been removed from several nuclear facilities on the eve of inspections. This set the stage for seven years of Iraqi concealment and evasion.

Rolf Ekeus has called UNSCOM's mission "the equivalent of war in arms control."

"To justify the absence of required data or documents, they offered stories that were the equivalent of 'the dog ate my homework,'" recounts weapons inspector Richard Butler. "One actual example: The wicked girlfriend of one of our workers tore up documents in anger. Another: A wandering psychopath cut some wires to the chemical-plant monitoring camera. It seems he hadn't received his medicine—because of the U.N. sanctions." On other occasions, in plain view of UNSCOM teams waiting to enter a weapons site, Iraqi trucks ferried incriminating documents in and out of the compound. In another, a weapons inspector seized a briefcase from Iraqi officials running out the back door of a laboratory—and found it contained test materials for anthrax and botulinim toxin. And, were it not for the 1995 defection of senior Iraqis, UNSCOM would never have made its most significant discoveries: that Iraq had manufactured and equipped weapons with the deadly chemical nerve agent VX and had an extensive biological warfare program. Nor were these isolated instances of Iraqi malfeasance. According to U.N. documents, "The highest level of concealment-related decisions are made by a small committee of high ranking officials. The committee directs the activities of a unit which is responsible for moving, hiding, and securing the items which are being concealed from the Commission."

Responsibility for punishing Iraqi violations lay, of course, with the United Nations. But not every member of the Security Council shared America's interest in disarming Iraq. France and Russia were particularly unhelpful. Both enjoyed extensive commercial ties with Baghdad and both delighted in frustrating U.S. foreign policy. Richard Butler recalls that when, in 1998, UNSCOM presented the Security Council with proof of Iraqi obstruction—including photos of Republican Guard trucks carrying away evidence—"French Ambassador Alain Dejammet speculated that perhaps a truckers' picnic was taking place." France and Russia also seized every opportunity to scale back the scope of the inspections regime, seconding Iraq's recommendation that UNSCOM inspectors be accompanied by diplomats (presumably theirs); refusing to accept the conclusions of UNSCOM reports; insisting that inspectors be more "culturally sensitive"; and, finally, condemning outright American efforts to punish Iraqi violations under the terms of Resolution 687.

Those efforts climaxed in November 1997, when Saddam ordered American members of UNSCOM out of Iraq. In reply, President Clinton ordered a buildup of U.S. forces in the Persian Gulf, and the Iraqi dictator seemed to back down. In early 1998, tensions flared up again when Saddam refused to allow weapons inspectors access to his many presidential palaces, which were suspected of housing evidence of Iraq's weapons programs. Russia and France threatened to veto any resolution that authorized force in response to the obstruction, and the United States prepared to act on its own. Once again, Iraq backed down. In August of 1998, however, Iraq announced that it was ending all cooperation with weapons inspectors. In November, it ended UNSCOM's remote monitoring of previously inspected facilities. A month later, without the support of France, Russia or U.N. Secretary General Kofi Annan—who had announced the previous February that Saddam was "a man I can do business with"—the United States launched Operation Desert Fox, a four-day fusillade of missiles directed at Republican Guard sites throughout Iraq. In response, Saddam refused to readmit the U.N. weapons inspectors he had ejected, and declared that the era of weapons inspections had ended. So too had UNSCOM.

The U.N., however, left the door slightly ajar. In January 2000, it established the United Nations Monitoring Verification and Inspection Commission (UNMOVIC), a sort of UNSCOM-lite. Under the terms of UNMOVIC, Iraq no longer had to eliminate its weapons of mass destruction in order to gain a reprieve from U.N. sanctions; it merely needed to demonstrate "cooperation." UNMOVIC was also designed to be "more aligned with the rest of the U.N. system, rather than being supported by the major Western countries"—another way of saying that it was designed to be less responsive to the United States' concerns about Saddam Hussein's predilection for doomsday weapons.

Under American pressure, UNMOVIC's mandate was strengthened in November 2002, and Saddam, facing the threat of war, decided to allow UNMOVIC teams back into the country. But as U.N. officials began their work, all signs were that Saddam would pick up where he left off in 1998, playing what defector Khidir Hamza calls "the same old game of hide and seek." Even if the inspectors do find evidence of weapons of mass destruction, that will only begin what the former deputy chairman of UNSCOM, Charles Duelfer, calls the "salami-slicing."

Whatever U.N. inspectors do or do not find, the fact remains that Saddam's WMD arsenal has gone unmonitored since 1998. Even then, UNSCOM was unable to account for a sizable chunk of Iraq's chemical, biological and nuclear inventory. According to figures from UNSCOM, the International Atomic Energy Agency and Richard Butler, compiled by the Wisconsin Project on Nuclear Arms Control in 1998, even after seven years of weapons inspections Saddam retained enough weapon-making material to wipe the Middle East off the map. Among the items that Iraq admitted to possessing, but which weapons inspectors could never locate, were: 3.9 tons of nerve gas, 600 tons of nerve gas ingredients, 550 artillery shells filled with mustard gas, 157 germ bombs, 25 missile warheads filled with anthrax and afla-toxin, and 50 Scud missile warheads. Then there are the items—such as components for at least three nuclear weapons and equipment to process nuclear-grade uranium—whose existence Iraq simply denied, though inspectors concluded otherwise. One of them, American weapons inspector Scott Ritter, summarized his findings in 1998: "Iraq has not disarmed, and they've lied across the board." His colleague Richard Butler recently told the Senate Foreign Relations Committee that, years of weapons inspections notwithstanding, "Iraq is well into CW [chemical weapons] production and may well be in the process of BW [biological weapons] production. With more than 10 tons of uranium and one ton of slightly enriched uranium, according to German intelligence, in its possession, Iraq has enough to generate the needed bomb-grade uranium for three nuclear weapons by 2005."

Or sooner. Following the Gulf War, U.N. inspectors found that Iraq was only months away from producing a nuclear bomb. We know that Saddam possesses the means, as outlined by UNSCOM, to rebuild his arsenal. According to a 2000 CIA report, "Since the suspension of U.N. inspections in December of 1998, Baghdad has had the capability to reinitiate both its CW and BW programs within a few weeks to months. After Desert Fox [the December 1998 U. S. strike], Baghdad again instituted a reconstruction effort on those facilities destroyed by the US bombing, including several critical missile production complexes and former dual-use CW production facilities."

Elaborating on this assessment, the outgoing secretary of defense, William Cohen, released a Pentagon report in January 2001 asserting that Iraq had rebuilt factories used to produce chemical and biological warfare agents. Then, in December of that year, a high-ranking Iraqi engineer named Adnan Saeed defected to the United States and told American officials about the locations and details of sites that Saddam was still using to store chemical, biological and nuclear materials. According to the *New York Times*, "Mr. Saeed said that several of the production and storage facilities were hidden in the rear of government companies and private villas in residential areas, or underground in what were built to look like water wells which are lined with lead-filled concrete and contain no water." Finally, in September 2002, the Bush administration and the British government presented further evidence that Iraq had been reconstituting its arsenal, including satellite photos and documents detailing Saddam's renewed effort to build long-range ballistic missiles. Finally, in December 2002, the U.N. inspection team reported that Iraq had failed to account for crucial elements of its deadly inventory.

The American Response

FOUR

Narrow Realism (Bush I)

How did the United States confront the threat posed by Saddam Hussein during the 1990s? On the whole, it did not. In the face of a tyrant bent on conquest and the acquisition of weapons of mass destruction, the first Bush and the Clinton administrations opted for a combination of incomplete military operations and diplomatic accommodation. Rather than press hard for a change of regime, President Bush halted the U.S. war against Iraq prematurely and turned a blind eye as Saddam slaughtered the insurgents whom the United States had encouraged to revolt. For its part, the Clinton administration avoided confronting the moral and strategic challenge presented by Saddam, hoping instead that an increasingly weak policy of containment, punctuated by the occasional fusillade of cruise missiles, would suffice to keep Saddam in his box.

At one level, the explanation for America's responses and non-responses to Iraqi provocations during the 1990s is fairly straight-forward. The past decade confounded the widespread, if much too sanguine, expectation that America's victory in the Gulf War would lead to the collapse of Saddam Hussein's regime. When this failed to happen, the Bush and Clinton administrations were then presented with a series of challenges that they could hardly have anticipated and to which they were obligated to respond as best they could. But neither administration was simply reacting on an ad hoc basis to events not of its making. The worldviews held by the Bush and Clinton teams shaped the way they dealt with Saddam. The fact that both administrations dealt with him so poorly underscores how defective their foreign policy approaches turned out to be.

Perhaps more than any other challenge facing the United States since the end of the Cold War, Iraq has become a template for various American approaches to the world. Among the truths our odd dance with Saddam has revealed is that U.S. foreign policy since the Cold War has been far from the incoherent muddle that critics routinely depict. On the contrary, each of the three post–Cold War presidencies has had its own fairly coherent worldview, each of which has been on display in America's dealings with Iraq.

The first Bush administration brought to the Middle East a worldview that prompted it to act aggressively in defense of our vital interests in Kuwait, but also left it wary of regime change in Baghdad and indifferent to the fate of Saddam's victims inside Iraq. This narrow realism descends from a brand of *realpolitik* which counsels that American foreign policy should be grounded in self-interest, narrowly understood. The Clinton team entered office with a very different worldview. Persuaded that America, after the Cold War, could achieve its foreign policy aims through commerce, diplomacy and negotiation, this administration embraced a kind of wishful liberalism that, in the case of Iraq, meant following the lead of the United Nations, employing American power fitfully and apologetically, often ignoring Saddam's challenges, and eventually presiding over the erosion of sanctions and weapons inspections.

During the first months of the current administration, George W. Bush seemed to oscillate between the policies of his predecessors, offering Iraq incentives for better behavior one day, and threats of punishment the next. Then Al Qaeda attacked. Within a few months, the Bush team had begun to articulate a view distinct from either of the two previous administrations. America's new strategy would in a sense combine the hardheaded approach of the first Bush administration with the moralism of the Clinton administration—reflecting what President Bush describes as "the union of our values and our national interests." The president had coined the term "distinctly American internationalism" for this worldview in his campaign. Now he began to act on it. And as with narrow realism and wishful liberalism before it, the substance of "distinctly American internationalism" will be tested in U.S. policy toward Iraq.

We hardly knew him. Or at least that was the excuse offered by U.S. officials when Saddam Hussein first came to the attention of the broad American public in 1990. There is a kernel of truth here, but no more. Though Saddam had been a player in Iraqi politics since 1968 and had ruled the country since 1979, it was only during the early 1980s that American officials became intimately acquainted with the dictator. Iraq, after all, had broken off relations with the United States in the aftermath of the 1967 Six-Day War, charging that Washington had been too supportive of Israel. Baghdad had also emerged as the Soviet Union's closest Arab ally. And Iraq's traditional rival, Iran, was—until the shah was deposed in 1979—a close friend to the United States.

All that changed in 1980 with the outbreak of the Iran-Iraq War. Initially, America's stance toward the conflict was one of studied neutrality. In fact, many U.S. policymakers greeted news of the hostilities with barely concealed glee. After all, here was a Soviet client state, on the one hand, waging war against a radical Islamic theocracy that was holding American hostages, on the other. The prevailing wisdom of the time was embodied in Henry Kissinger's comment, "It is too bad they both can't lose." That sentiment, however, generally gave way to a pro-Iraq tilt during the first years of the Reagan administration. When it came to Khomeini's Iran, the logic of "the enemy of my enemy is my friend" proved too compelling to resist. And the Reagan administration hoped to wean Iraq away from the Soviet Union—a hope that Saddam bolstered by curtailing his ties to Moscow.

By 1982, America's tilt began yielding concrete benefits for Iraq, as the Reagan team removed Iraq from its roster of terror sponsors. A year later, Undersecretary of State Lawrence Eagleburger sent a letter to Export-Import Bank chairman William Draper "to bring to your attention the important role EXIM can play in furthering long-range political and economic interests of the United States" by lending to Iraq, while Vice President George Bush added that "Eximbank could play a crucial role in our efforts in the region." By the end of the year, the United States was supplying Saddam with hundreds of millions of dollars in credits, and by 1987 over half a billion dollars annually. Nor was that all. A 1983 National Security Council study, leaked to the *New York Times,* suggested that the United States "encourage other countries to arm and finance Iraq's war effort." In 1984, the United States and Iraq resumed diplomatic relations, and the list of items that America was exporting to Saddam promptly expanded to include technology and materials some feared might be useful for weapons of mass destruction. Concerns about their possible military use gave the White House little pause. According to Bruce Jentleson, talking points prepared for a 1987 meeting between Vice President Bush and the Iraqi ambassador stressed that delays in shipping these items were "capricious" and that "a special look" would be taken to see whether the delays could be eliminated. Among the items that the Reagan team would eventually ship to Iraq were bacteria, missile system components and explosives technology.

The relationship between Baghdad and Washington was hardly a reciprocal one. Saddam was already well known for his execrable conduct at home and abroad, and American influence did nothing to moderate it. Not that the Reagan administration made much of an attempt to do so. Despite the warnings of administration officials like Zalmay Khalilzad and Richard Perle, who cautioned that "Iraq is a problem country" which "continues to actively pursue an interest in nuclear weapons," the engagement with Saddam continued apace. Despite Iraq's willingness to host Abu Abbas, ringleader of the 1985 Achille Lauro hijacking, where terrorists dumped a wheelchair-bound American into the sea, Secretary of State George Shultz insisted that "Iraq has effectively disassociated itself from international terrorism," and the administration resisted congressional pressure to return Iraq to its terrorism list. And despite overwhelming evidence that Saddam was gassing the Kurds, the Reagan administration opposed congressional efforts to sanction Iraq. Finally, despite a 1987 Iraqi missile attack on the USS *Stark* that claimed the lives of thirty-seven American sailors, the administration readily accepted Saddam's explanation that the attack was a mistake. In these and other efforts, the administration was buttressed by the arguments of, among others, the U.S. Chamber of Commerce, which urged that detractors of Saddam Hussein "set aside the emotions of the moment," and Washington's think-tank community, one of whose "experts" glimpsed over the horizon the possibility of a "perestroika in Iraq."

During the first two years of his administration, President George H. W. Bush continued the Iraq policy of the Reagan years, which was to deal with Saddam Hussein more or less without condition and regardless of consequence. With the Iran-Iraq War having ended in August 1988, the rationale for supporting Saddam—"the enemy of my enemy is my friend"—should have seemed less compelling. Nonetheless, the Bush team pressed ahead, convinced that a conciliatory approach toward the dictator could bring Iraq into the "family of nations" and that Iraq could become "a more responsible, status-quo state working within the system, and promoting stability in the region." To this end, Bush expanded the flow of subsidies, agricultural aid and advanced technology to Iraq (over the objections of his own Commerce Department). And when, in 1989, the Agriculture Department, the Treasury and the Federal Reserve suggested that aid should be halted, Secretary of State James Baker, his deputy, Lawrence Eagleburger, and National Security Council advisor Brent Scowcroft all weighed in against them. On the question of what leverage the United States could bring to bear to modify Saddam's behavior at home and abroad, the Bush team was without illusions. "Our efforts should concentrate on slow, steady pressure and realistic appraisal of our leverage," argued a White House policy paper. "We should ... be realistic and demand of Iraq what we do of its neighbors—in tune with our aim to rope Iraq into a conservative and responsible alignment in foreign policy." As for the Kurds, who were at that moment being slaughtered, the paper added, with italics to emphasize the point, that *"in no way should we associate ourselves with the 60-year-old rebellion in Iraq or oppose Iraq's legitimate attempts to suppress it."*

Lest anyone in the bureaucracy mistake the direction of U.S. policy, in October 1989, President Bush issued National Security Directive 26, which ordered the different branches of the federal government to expand America's political and economic ties to Baghdad. Not a month later, according to a declassified State Department report, intelligence officials reported that Iraq was diverting dual-use American exports to military projects and using front companies to acquire nuclear technology. Undeterred, Baker's State Department and Scowcroft's NSC secured $1 billion in loan guarantees for Iraq that same month. And when, early the next year, the Voice of America editorialized against Saddam's human rights violations, Baker became apoplectic, ordering all future VOA editorials to be cleared by State, and cabling the U.S. ambassador in Iraq, April Glaspie, "it is in no way USG [U.S. Government] policy to suggest that the Government of Iraq is illegitimate or that the people of Iraq should or will revolt against the Government of Iraq." Glaspie immediately wrote the Iraqi foreign minister a letter insisting that "President Bush wants good relations with Iraq, relations built on confidence and trust, so that we can discuss a broad range of issues frankly and fruitfully. I am sorry that the Government of Iraq did not inform me of its concern about the editorial sooner, so that I could have provided you with the official assurance of our regret without delay." A Senate delegation, including Republican leaders Robert Dole and Alan Simpson, reinforced the message on a trip to Baghdad a month later. "I believe your problem is with the Western media, not with the U.S. government," Simpson groveled. "The press is spoiled and conceited ... they do not want to see anything succeeding or achieving its objectives. My advice is that you allow those bastards to come here and see things for themselves." Having seen things for himself, Simpson returned to Washington, where, echoing the administration's line, he opposed congressional bills that would have sanctioned Iraq for Saddam's human rights violations.

Up to the eve of the Gulf War, the Bush team continued trying to work with Saddam. Neither Saddam's threats to incinerate Israel, his bellicose stance toward Kuwait, nor even his increasingly strident anti-American rhetoric budged the president from his hopes for the Iraqi dictator. On the contrary: In response to Iraqi troop movements along the border with Kuwait, the State Department dispatched Ambassador Glaspie to mollify Saddam. At a July 25, 1990 meeting, the Iraqi leader predicted to Glapsie that America would not oppose his aims because "yours is a society that cannot accept 10,000 dead in one battle." To which Glaspie replied, "we have no opinion on the Arab-Arab conflicts like your border disagreement with Kuwait. . . . James Baker has directed our official spokesman to emphasize this instruction."

Back in Washington, even State Department officials were appalled. So the administration tried again. The task of replying to

Saddam's outburst, however, fell to State Department and NSC officials who still believed in the Iraqi dictator. Principal among these was Richard Haass, the NSC's Middle East point man. Despite the fact that Saddam's troops continued to mass on the Kuwaiti border, Haass, according to Michael Gordon and Bernard Trainor's account in *The Generals' War,* "saw the presidential message as an opportunity to acknowledge the easing of the tensions and reaffirm the policy of moderation." This he did by helping to craft a message from Bush, which the president sent to Saddam. "Let me assure you, as my Ambassador, Senator Dole and others have done," the president wrote on July 28, "that my Administration continues to desire better relations with Iraq. We will also continue to support our other friends in the region with whom we have had long-standing ties. We see no necessary inconsistency between these two objectives." Saddam's reply came four days later, when he invaded Kuwait.

Bush's declaration, soon after the invasion, that Saddam's aggression "will not stand" brought the Bush team together behind a new policy. Or almost together. The chairman of the Joint Chiefs of Staff, Colin Powell, thought the president's statement was premature, and complained that he had not been consulted first. In the war's aftermath, Lawrence Eagleburger insisted, "I know personally that if Colin had had his druthers we would not have fought the Iraq war. President Bush and Brent Scowcroft pushed him into it." This appears to have been true from the outset. First, Powell opposed a show of naval force to deter the threatened invasion. When the invasion did occur, Powell steadfastly argued against reversing it. "The American people do not want their young dying for $1.50 gallon oil," Powell declared in internal deliberations. "We can't make a case for losing lives for Kuwait." Writing about the arguments of Powell and others, Scowcroft recounts that he "was frankly appalled at the undertone of the discussion, which suggested resignation to the invasion and even adaptation to a fait accompli."

Despite the reluctance of the Joint Chiefs chairman to go to war against Iraq, the president acted to restore Kuwait's sovereignty. But the war aims were focused on expelling Saddam from Kuwait, and Powell in particular was eager to enforce this limitation. The day after the ground offensive began, he was already pressing for its end. After only four days of fighting, when American units had yet to encircle Iraqi forces, Powell convinced President Bush to halt ground operations. "The vaunted Republican Guard formations are no longer," the general announced. He was wrong. Their escape routes clear, three largely intact Republican Guard divisions escaped back to Iraq—where some of them began massacring Iraqi civilians whom the United States had encouraged to revolt. At the White House, Secretary of State Baker, too, argued for a halt to the American advance. "We have done the job. We can stop. We have achieved our aims. We have gotten them out of Kuwait."

On the ground, the situation looked a bit different. General Norman Schwarzkopf recommended continuing the assault, arguing that he needed at least another day to destroy the armored units that would later be turned against the Kurds and the Shiites. Nonetheless, Bush agreed with Powell and Baker, and after a hundred hours of fighting he called an end to ground operations.

In fact, the decision to end the war once Iraqi forces were driven from Kuwait had been taken two months before. At a December 1990 White House meeting, according to Brent Scowcroft, the Bush administration decided not to aim for Saddam's removal. As the national security advisor recounts in the memoir he co-authored with the president, *A World Transformed,* "We would be committing ourselves—alone—to removing one regime and installing another and if the Iraqis themselves didn't take matters into their own hands, we would be facing . . . some dubious 'nation-building.'" There was also the fear that toppling Saddam could end in the splintering of Iraq—an outcome that Baker described as the "Lebanonization of Iraq." Echoing Baker, Powell wrote in his own memoir, "It would not contribute to the stability we want in the Middle East to have Iraq fragmented into separate Sunni, Shia, and Kurd political entities." Moreover, he recalled, "our practical intention was to leave Baghdad enough power to survive as a threat to an Iran that remained bitterly hostile to the United States." What the Bush team wanted, in short, was Iraqi "stability"—even if it had to be enforced by Saddam Hussein.

In Iraq's southern marshes and in its northern mountains, the human cost of the Bush team's narrow *realpolitik* rapidly became clear. Relying on the Republican Guard divisions that had escaped from

Kuwait and on helicopter gunships, which the Bush team had for some reason exempted from its prohibition on Iraqi military flights, Saddam proceeded to slaughter thousands of Kurds and Shiites. "I frankly wish [the uprising] hadn't happened," Scowcroft later recalled. "I envisioned a postwar government being a military government." For his part, Bush claimed that "for very practical reasons there was never a promise to aid an uprising." But he had repeatedly and openly encouraged a revolt, exhorting "the Iraqi people to take matters into their own hands and force Saddam Hussein, the dictator, to step aside." When the Iraqi people tried to do exactly that, the United States turned a blind eye as they were ruthlessly put down, sometimes within sight of American armored units.

In his memoirs, Powell mocks the notion that "if Saddam had fallen, he would necessarily have been replaced by a Jeffersonian in some sort of desert democracy where people read *The Federalist Papers* along with the Koran." But the issue was not whether Iraqi rebels had any use for *The Federalist Papers;* it was simply whether to stand with those we had encouraged to overthrow Saddam Hussein's regime. In the end, the Bush administration's commitment to "stability" trumped any inclination to aid those Iraqis who rebelled against their dictator with American encouragement and in the name of American principles.

The set of beliefs—we call them narrow realism—that structured the Bush team's decisions (and failures, we would assert) in Iraq and elsewhere created precedents that would shackle the next president and the one after that. To be fair, one must acknowledge that the Bush policy toward Iraq reflected a strong current in American foreign policy thinking. That point of view was proud to use terms like "realpolitik" or "realism" in describing itself. Though ostensibly a method of analysis that eschews ideology, realism had by the time of the Bush presidency become an ideology of its own, one which counseled that foreign policy should be grounded only in vital interests, not ideals or abstract principles. Bush heeded that counsel in dealing with China, the Soviet Union, Yugoslavia and, of course, Iraq. This worldview continues to be embraced by much of the foreign policy establishment, which remains wary of an overly moralistic American presence on the international scene. Poring over maps and position papers, these narrow realists never tire of cautioning policy-makers about the perils of devising foreign policy on the basis of what they deride as "moralism" rather than concrete interest.

At first glance, this repudiation of principle might seem contrary to American temperament. In their defense, the adherents of realism trace its American roots back to early American statesmen such as John Quincy Adams, who famously said that America "goes not abroad, in search of monsters to destroy. She is the well-wisher to the freedom and independence of all. She is the champion and vindicator only of her own." Yet the brand of realism popularized in the United States after the Second World War and still in vogue today owes more to the unsentimental *realpolitik* practiced by nineteenth-century European statesmen like Bismarck and Metternich—and articulated by their twentieth-century intellectual heirs in Europe and in America—than it does to our Founding Fathers.

Arguing against the "moralistic" strain in U.S. foreign policy, these thinkers advocated a policy based on what the father of academic realism, Hans Morgenthau, identified as "interests defined in terms of power." Morgenthau condemned the effort to apply a nation's principles abroad as itself evidence of "immorality," neatly exemplified "in the contemporary phenomenon of the moral crusade." Rather, the realists argued, a hardheaded acceptance of a balance of power between states as existed in nineteenth-century Europe would be more likely to restrain nations' bellicose impulses than would an attempt to improve the world. This in turn led to the realists' key recommendation: A state must limit itself to the protection of its "vital interests," lest it disrupt the balance of power.

The realist obsession with "vital interests" never fully jibed with America's definition of its national interest, which even in the era of the Founders included more than purely material or geographic considerations. "Repudiation of Europe," novelist John Dos Passos once said, "is, after all, America's main excuse for being." Repudiating Europe, however, is exactly the opposite of what the realists had in mind. As a result, they failed to take note of the special appeal and power of American, versus, say, Soviet ideals. This became particularly apparent during the Nixon presidency, when Henry Kissinger argued against "the illusion of simple solutions" to the problem of Soviet communism. Kissinger sought instead to maintain a balance of power, and to secure a "détente," between Washington and Moscow. Accordingly, he opposed efforts to press for the improvement of human rights and political freedoms in the Soviet Union, and struggled for years to instruct Americans on the futility of efforts to "transform the Soviet system by pressure." But while the United States may have been following Kissinger's admonitions about "restraint in the uses of power, and abstention from efforts to exploit instability or local conflicts," the Soviets, as Kissinger himself now concedes, were not. And the Soviets' steady ideological and geographic advances were one reason that narrow realism came under broad assault in the 1976 election.

From the left, Kissinger's approach was condemned by Jimmy Carter, a Vietnam-era liberal who found power politics so repugnant that his foreign policy shied away from promoting anything resembling a national interest. From the right, realism was repudiated in 1976 by candidate Ronald Reagan, a staunch anticommunist who saw no contradiction between the assertion of American power and American ideals.

First Carter's approach, then Reagan's, dominated the next twelve years. But with the end of the Cold War, which coincided with the presidency of George Herbert Walker Bush, narrow realism made a comeback. Members of the Bush team, David Halberstam writes approvingly, saw the Cold War as "an ongoing conflict between two superpowers," unlike the Reagan team, which saw it as "a clash between good and evil." With the globe convulsed by change, Bush, whose disdain for "moral crusades" reflected foreign policy inclinations that put him closer to Gerald Ford than to Ronald Reagan, placed a premium on the maintenance of "stability." But the Soviet Union was gone, and in the absence of a rival superpower, "stability" came to mean something quite different than it had in a bipolar world where it had assumed, at minimum, an American willingness to check the Soviet Union.

At times, the Bush team's desire for stability even led it to consider propping up regimes whose demise Americans might be expected to cheer. "I was skeptical about the wisdom of pursuing German unification," Bush national security advisor Brent Scowcroft recalls. "What was wrong with a divided Germany as long as the situation was stable? The very process of unification could be extremely destabilizing, and could even lead to conflict." This preference for order over liberty extended to Hungary, Czechoslovakia and Poland, whose dictator, Wojciech Jaruzelski, Bush found "charming." It even extended to the Soviet Union itself, where the Bush team embraced communist leader Mikhail Gorbachev and was suspicious of the opposition movement led by Boris Yeltsin. Indeed, Scowcroft found it "painful to watch Yeltsin rip the Soviet Union brick by brick away from Gorbachev." The concern for the Soviet Union's welfare led Bush in 1991 to warn the Ukrainian people, in what would soon become known as the "Chicken Kiev speech," that America would "not support those who seek independence in order to replace a far-off tyranny with a local despotism." The Soviet Union collapsed anyway.

This was not the only instance when Bush's "realistic" disdain for the "vision thing" was painfully apparent. In China, the Bush team reacted to pro-democracy marches and the massacre in Tiananmen Square by excusing the communist regime in Beijing. As the president confided in his diary a month after Tiananmen, there was "nothing that I really want China to do in order to solve the existing problem of strained relations." The "problem," in the Bush team's view, was our own. Hence, Bush dispatched Scowcroft and Undersecretary of State Eagleburger on a secret journey to Beijing in July 1989 to patch things up—followed by yet another trip where the two officials exchanged toasts with their Chinese hosts. Bush then vetoed legislation allowing Chinese students to prolong their stays in the United States, pressed to remove sanctions, and made other conciliatory gestures to Beijing.

In Yugoslavia, where Slobodan Milosevic had begun to pursue a policy of ethnic cleansing, the Bush team's response was much the same. Justifying American inaction, Bush likened the war in the Balkans to a "hiccup." Or as David Gompert, then a U.S. official working on Bosnia, put it: "Following the Gulf War, a leading role in Yugoslavia would have implied that the United States could and would act as international policeman." This was something the Bush administration had vowed it would not do. Hence, Secretary of State James Baker, who spent months shuttling back and forth to jumpstart the Middle East "peace process," spent exactly a day in Belgrade trying to forestall the coming catastrophe. "Milosevic had Saddam's appetite," Baker recounts in his memoir, "but Serbia didn't have Iraq's capabilities." So America overlooked his aggression, instead declaring itself wedded to the "territorial integrity" of Yugoslavia. No matter that the Bush team had put its faith in the "territorial integrity" of a state that no longer existed; "We don't have a dog in that fight," Baker insisted.

It was in Iraq, however, that the Bush team's foreign policy philosophy manifested itself clearly—and at greater moral cost—than anywhere else. Its members still defend their "realistic" approach toward Saddam. But exactly how realistic was the decision to coddle an aggressive dictator in the weeks, months and years before he invaded Kuwait? And, in the aftermath of the Gulf War, how realistic was the preference for a stable Iraq under Saddam Hussein as opposed to the nontyrannical alternative? According to the worldview of the Bush team, the decisions all made perfect sense. "The Lebanonization of Iraq," "nation-building," "some sort of desert democracy where people read *The Federalist Papers* along with the Koran"—these were the phrases that justified halting the Gulf War prematurely and looking aside while Iraqis were slaughtered by the thousands. Twelve years later, as Saddam threatens the region and the world with weapons of mass destruction, we are still living with the consequences of such "realism."

FIVE

Wishful Liberalism (Clinton)

Oddly enough, given what would soon follow, candidate Bill Clinton attacked the Bush team for having "failed to learn from its appeasement of Saddam Hussein" and for having "left the Kurds and the Shiites twisting." His administration, by contrast, would not "forge strategic relationships with dangerous, despotic regimes." The new administration pledged to "contain" the Iraqi dictator with vigilant enforcement of U.N. sanctions and a steady stream of aid to Iraqi opposition forces. In August 1993, Vice President Gore wrote to the Iraqi National Congress affirming America's "solid commitment" to "your struggle" and pledging that the Clinton team "will not turn our backs." They would not turn their backs, explained Clinton's Middle East point man at the NSC, Martin Indyk, because "Our purpose is deliberate: it is to establish clearly and unequivocally that the current regime in Iraq is a criminal regime, beyond the pale of international society and, in our judgment, irredeemable."

The Clinton team would act on this purpose by providing millions of dollars in aid to the Iraqi opposition, assistance from the CIA, meetings with Gore, Secretary of State Warren Christopher and national security advisor Anthony Lake, and promises of still more help to come. Taking these assurances to heart, Iraqi opposition forces launched an offensive in the spring of 1995 and bested two of Saddam's crack army divisions. Fearing, however, that the assault might embroil the United States in a major confrontation with Iraq, the White House abruptly ordered the CIA to withdraw its support and warned Kurdish leaders directly that "the United States will not support this operation militarily or in any other way." In newspaper

interviews, members of the Clinton team spun the betrayal as a calculated decision based on the ineptitude of the opposition force.
"These guys are a feckless bunch who couldn't hold up a 7-Eleven,"
said one. "They are really more gnats and mosquitoes to Saddam
rather than anything serious," echoed another. The administration's
about-face concluded in 1996 when Saddam invaded the northern
Kurdish "safe haven" that the United States had pledged to safeguard.
Far from protecting its inhabitants, American officials fleeing ahead
of the offensive left behind scores of the Iraqi leaders they had been
working with, at least 100 of whom were executed on the spot. In the
midst of the slaughter, Secretary of Defense William Perry explained,
"Our interest in the Kurds is not a vital national security interest."

Part of the problem with U.S. policy toward Iraq was simply
ambivalence about the use of force as an instrument of policy. For
members of the Clinton team, the value of American power seemed
to lay merely in its capacity to influence Saddam, to prod him to see
the error of his ways. Thus, terms like "signals" and "messages"—pre-
sumed after Vietnam to have been banished forever from the lexicon
of military affairs—returned to favor in this administration's dealings with Iraq. "Our missiles sent the following message to Saddam
Hussein," remarked the president in his statement announcing a 1996
strike in retaliation for Saddam's aggression in northern Iraq. "When
you abuse your own people or threaten your neighbors, you must pay
a price." Missiles would inform Saddam that his meddling in northern Iraq was unacceptable, letting him know, according to President
Clinton, "that reckless acts have consequences." In this, the strike
resembled nothing so much as Clinton's 1993 missile attack on a
Baghdad intelligence facility in response to the assassination attempt
on former President Bush. That attack, according to U.N. ambassador Madeleine Albright, was "a message directed at Iraq . . . a message
about terrorism and the fact that we will not allow it." But as Vice
President Gore hastened to add, "It was not designed to bring down
the regime of Saddam Hussein."

Clinton's sudden enthusiasm for stand-off missile attacks against
Iraq was ironic. After all, the Clinton national security team had entered
office persuaded of the merits of "assertive multilateralism," a doctrine
based on employing American power in concert with and on behalf

of the international community. But the fiasco leading to the deaths of U.S. Rangers in Somalia, where the Clinton team had placed U.S. troops at the U.N.'s disposal, demolished the appeal of this theory. More than that, it obliged Clinton to endure public ridicule—both for expanding the mission in Somalia and for precipitously withdrawing U.S. troops after the firefight. Subsequently, the White House retreated to another liberal paradigm for the use of force: a doctrine permitting aggressive military measures only against inanimate objects.

With its pinprick strikes against Iraq, however, the administration invited Americans to indulge in the conceit that the United States needed no grand strategy in dealing with Iraq, that its military prowess obviated the need to think seriously about purpose and policy. Hence, in responding to the Iraqi attack on the northern city of Irbil in 1996 by pummeling air defense sites scattered about the desert south of Baghdad, the Clinton team was not behaving the least bit illogically. Hardly had the missiles struck their targets when the administration began making the case that the action was a huge success. "Our mission has been achieved," Clinton declared within twenty-four hours of the first strike, citing reports that "there has been a withdrawal of the forces, a dispersal of the forces" to bolster his claim. Nor did the ensuing strategic upheaval in northern Iraq and the near-collapse of the allied coalition persuade the president to budge from that claim. In fact, a comparable disconnect between claims and reality characterized almost every attack against Iraq that the administration launched. Although it had only destroyed part of one building along with its janitorial staff, the administration had declared its 1993 strike "a devastating blow to Iraq's ability to plan and carry out [terrorist] operations in the future," in the words of Vice President Gore. If blowing holes in a building counted as a "devastating blow," it was also cheap, an after-hours missile attack that not only precluded American casualties but, as Secretary of State Warren Christopher hastened to point out, also sought to "minimize the loss of [Iraqi] life." The strikes, however, did not modify Saddam's behavior in the least, but rather showed him that he enjoyed more room to maneuver than American rhetoric suggested.

That this was the "message" that Saddam received from U.S. policy became particularly clear during Clinton's second term. Rhetorically, the administration accepted the goal of regime change in Iraq, and in response to Saddam's defiance of U.N. weapons inspectors, the White House ordered numerous ostentatious buildups of U.S. forces in the Gulf during 1997 and 1998, accompanied by leaked details about the ominous comings and goings of aircraft carriers and the movement of warplanes. As the pattern evolved, the administration would devise a fig leaf to allow it to back down from the real action these buildups seemed to portend. Then the process would begin anew. An early 1998 confrontation with Saddam exposed the true extent of the Clinton team's confusion. When Saddam refused to submit to further weapons inspections in late 1997, Clinton vowed that if force was required this time, the United States would "eliminate" Iraq's capacity to produce weapons of mass destruction. Yet even as the U.S. buildup proceeded, the administration reverted to type. In order to insure the elimination of Iraq's WMD program, would the administration use ground forces? Absolutely not. Could air power destroy Saddam's weapons? Not really, given that he had buried and hidden so much of his arsenal. So the White House argued itself into a "surgical" campaign of only four or five days, which would at most "diminish" Iraqi capabilities.

As Clinton administration officials repeatedly reminded the public (and Saddam), any use of military power against Iraq would be designed to minimize the risk of casualties (whether ours or theirs), avoid collateral damage, preclude the danger of a "quagmire," skirt moral ambiguities, and achieve its desired effect through suasion rather than overwhelming force. Thus, the Clinton administration insisted that such an attack was not to be confused with waging war, a concept that was antiquated and obsolete. "We are talking about using military force, but we are not talking about a war," Secretary of State Madeleine Albright argued. "That is an important distinction." But the administration's insistence upon such distinctions, along with the lengthening list of criteria to be met before military force was used, fatally undercut its position. After all the huffing and puffing was over, Albright flew to New York to cut a deal with Kofi Annan that would permit the United States to back down.

Finally, in December 1998, when Saddam's manipulations became too much to bear, the Clinton team responded with another round of missile strikes. Severely limited in purpose, scope, duration and effect, the days-long campaign produced nothing—apart from the collapse of weapons inspections. Indeed, the Iraqi dictator emerged stronger than before. As a result, during Clinton's final year in office, Iraq exported more oil than any other country save Saudi Arabia, earned more from oil sales than it did prior to the embargo, and used those earnings to help replenish its arsenal.

As for Saddam's opponents, with the administration's approval Marine Corps General Anthony Zinni, commander of U.S. forces in the Middle East, launched a public relations offensive against them, arguing further in speeches and interviews that "a weak, fragmented, chaotic Iraq . . . is more dangerous in the long run than a contained Saddam is now." For his part, Clinton's national security advisor, Sandy Berger, publicly likened plans to topple Saddam to another Bay of Pigs, and the White House released only a tiny portion of the funds Congress had allotted to support the opposition. Instead, the State Department funded such pressing needs as a conflict management program for Saddam's opponents established by Roger Fisher, the author of *Getting to Yes.*

In fact, the very officials responsible for supporting Saddam's opponents routinely denigrated them. On the strength of an article in which he argued that rolling back Saddam Hussein was a "fantasy," Berger brought former CIA analyst Kenneth Pollack onto the National Security Council. According to the *Washington Post,* Pollack had authored intelligence estimates that "predicted fierce and effective Iraqi resistance" prior to Operation Desert Storm, and, by his own account, once inside the Clinton administration he "stopped trying to convince anyone that the [Iraqi National Congress] was worth assisting." In a similar vein, Frank Ricciardone, the State Department coordinator responsible for implementing the Iraq Liberation Act, said the United States would not supply arms to the Iraqi opposition until "we know that they represent fighters who are willing to die" for regime change.

Meanwhile, in 2000, Baghdad's newly reopened Saddam International Airport began disgorging a steady stream of politicians and businessmen on unauthorized flights from Russia, France and the Arab world. All were there to do business with the outlaw regime.

Washington not only failed to condemn the wholesale subversion of the U.N. sanctions, but negotiated with the U.N. Sanctions Committee to revise the rules governing flights into Iraq so it would not appear that the embargo was being violated. While all this was going on, members of the Gulf War coalition one after another reopened their embassies in Baghdad, sent dignitaries to commune with Saddam, and lamented the injustice and immorality of sanctions.

In this atmosphere of slow-motion capitulation, the United States agreed with the move to abolish altogether the U.N.-imposed ceiling on Iraqi oil sales, winking at the fact that outside the auspices of the United Nations, Baghdad was smuggling out an additional $2 billion of oil a year. On the military front, as soon as the 1998 strikes ceased, Berger and Albright pressed to ratchet down the war of attrition in which U.S. warplanes had been engaged since the Gulf War. But Iraqi jets continued to challenge the no-fly zones and Iraqi gunners continued to shoot at American planes. So the air campaign continued, but it did so in a curious way: The Pentagon devised a strategy whereby the Air Force would fill 2,000-pound bombs with concrete instead of explosives and drop them on Iraq. "The guidance equipment is still there, but the cement is less expensive," explained Lieutenant Colonel Michael Waters, spokesman for the allied air operation over northern Iraq. But cost was not the only reason the United States was bombarding Iraq with construction materials. "The way we're conducting this is kept within the parameters of political acceptability," an administration official told the *New York Times*. "We don't want things to go wrong."

But things went wrong anyway. How badly wrong was clear in the administration's determination to avoid another showdown with Saddam over weapons inspections. "During a conversation about the regime change plan in early 2000," writes former Clinton administration official Kenneth Pollack, "one senior administration official told me that 'The President wants to finish his term by making peace between the Arabs and the Israelis, he doesn't want to start a war between us and the Iraqis.'" This desire was complicated in the fall of 2000 when the new chief U.N. weapons inspector, Hans Blix, planned to announce that his team was ready to return to Iraq. The declaration was long overdue: "In the absence of inspectors on the ground," Assistant Secretary of State Edward Walker said at the time, "we must rely on national technical means, which cannot provide the same level of assurance." Yet the administration, intent on avoiding a confrontation, scuttled Blix's plan. A U.N. diplomat told the *Washington Post* that the decision to obstruct Blix derived from U.S. as well as Russian concerns "that this might create a climate of confrontation at an inappropriate time." Indeed, Secretary of State Albright publicly ruled out the use of force in response to Saddam's intransigence. "There seem to be many people who are guessing that not much might happen before the American elections," Blix commented after his travel plans were altered. "I think that might be a good guess."

Opponents of Clinton's foreign policy, loath to credit the administration with coherence in any enterprise apart from campaigning for reelection, dismiss any suggestion that the administration's policy in Iraq evidenced consistency. But such a view is mistaken. When the Bush team departed office in January 1993, taking with it the philosophy of foreign policy realism, Bill Clinton criticized his predecessor for failing to grasp that "in a world where freedom, not tyranny, is on the march, the cynical calculus of pure power politics simply does not compute." In its place, Clinton pledged to conduct a foreign policy that rejected this cynical calculus. He would start with Saddam Hussein, about whom a newly inaugurated President Clinton said, "I believe in death-bed conversions."

What Clinton was proposing was, in short, the very opposite of realism. Instead, he was guided by a brand of wishful liberalism, a view that looks to the world community and its institutions as the ultimate source of international legitimacy, is profoundly uncomfortable with the unilateral assertion of American power, and tends to favor policies that rely far more heavily on the carrot than on the stick. As expressed in arms control agreements, international treaties, and an aversion to the use of force, this impulse has translated into a preference for a foreign policy whose idealism is both quixotic and legalistic. In the past, it has also shaded into utopianism, contributing to, among other highlights of U.S. foreign policy, the creation of the League of Nations, the 1928 Kellogg-Briand Pact outlawing war, and a persistent faith in Cold War arms control treaties that were persistently violated by the Soviet Union.

This strain of liberalism was kept in check during the first two decades of the Cold War by the dominance of muscular liberals like Harry Truman and John F. Kennedy, who harbored no illusions about the perils that existed beyond America's shores. But the liberal foreign policy consensus evaporated in the jungles of Vietnam. For wishful liberals, and many others besides, American power was now irredeemably tainted by involvement in a "criminal" war. The suspicion of American power inherent in contemporary liberalism now became a reflexive opposition to the exercise of American power in the world. That sentiment soon became common among some leaders of the Democratic Party. In 1972, Democratic presidential nominee George McGovern was caustically depicting the American effort in Vietnam as "a policy of mass murder" and demanding that America "come home" from Southeast Asia and the world. And while such bluntness tended to be the exception rather than the norm, by the early 1970s a conventional wisdom had emerged among many liberal foreign policy types: Not only did the United States share equal responsibility for the origins, excesses and consequences of the Cold War, but its international conduct was barely different from that of its communist adversary.

This reflexive suspicion of American power would be enshrined in the Democratic Party's platform in 1972 and would shape opinion in its salons for the next two decades. President Carter thus congratulated America for having overcome its "inordinate fear of communism" as well as the "belief that Soviet expansion was almost inevitable and that it must be contained." Liberals during the 1970s would terminate aid to South Vietnam and to pro-Western insurgents in Africa, and preside over successive catastrophes in Afghanistan, Central America and Iran. With the Cold War approaching its end game, Democratic congressmen such as David Bonior, Jim Wright and Christopher Dodd spent much of the 1980s directing the successful drive to defund the Sandinistas' anticommunist opponents. Aptly summarizing this position, Senator Dodd advised that, when it came to communist advances in Central America, the United States "had to move with the tide of history rather than stand against it." Similarly, in 1984 presidential nominee Walter Mondale impugned President Reagan for policies that "ceded the moral high ground to the Russians." And in 1988 presidential nominee Michael Dukakis assailed efforts to assist the Contras, and denounced the bombing of Libya and the invasion of Grenada.

Communism died, but these liberal qualms about American power persisted. What had begun as opposition to the war in Vietnam had, by the end of the Cold War, hardened into a reflexive opposition to the use of force. Libya, Iran, Iraq—the ideology of those who identified themselves as America's foes no longer mattered. The Gulf War, fought more than a year after the fall of the Berlin Wall, elicited all the old arguments. Senator Robert Kerrey, for instance, advised that "rather than threatening war . . . we should tell Iraq and the world we believe the wholesale loss of American and Arab lives is too great a price to pay to liberate Kuwait," while even moderates like Senators Sam Nunn and Daniel Patrick Moynihan could not discern a compelling reason to back the use of force against Iraqi aggression. A year later, Democratic senators like Ted Kennedy and Joseph Biden were once again in full cry, condemning a leaked Bush administration report that explained how America could retain its military primacy. California senator Alan Cranston sneered that the memo's purpose was to make the United States "the one, the only main honcho on the world block, the global Big Enchilada."

During the 1992 Democratic primaries, as well, the presidential candidates recited the familiar litany. Paul Tsongas lectured that Americans cannot "allow ourselves to continually become the policeman of the world." And Tom Harkin advised voters, "If you want to carry on spending your money overseas, then vote for George Herbert Walker Bush." For his part, Bill Clinton championed the creation of a "new, voluntary U.N. Rapid Deployment Force" that could alleviate America's burdens abroad.

Although President Clinton's foreign policy may not have been the product of principled analysis, it did reflect certain assumptions about America's role in the world. Clinton, of course, entered the White House pledging to "focus like a laser" on the domestic economy. This had a direct bearing on foreign policy, for as Peter Tarnoff, Clinton's undersecretary of state for policy, explained, "we simply don't have the leverage, we don't have the influence, we don't have the inclination to use military forces, we certainly don't have the money" to settle global crises. Hence, the administration's early inaction on Bosnia—whose destruction the Clinton administration regretted but for almost three years did little to stop—signaled the arrival of a foreign policy premised, in Tarnoff's words, on "setting limits on the amount of American engagement." To this end, the Clinton administration looked to the United Nations and a doctrine of "assertive multilateralism" because, as the president explained, "We've simply got to focus on rebuilding America." Cheering the president on, the *New York Times* advised that "the new administration also needs to ease America out of the costly role of world policeman by helping to transform the United Nations and regional groups into credible instruments for enforcing collective security." This the administration proceeded to do by preparing a Presidential Decision Directive that amounted to a blueprint for subordinating American power to the judgment of the United Nations. Defense Secretary William Perry captured its spirit a year later, solemnly explaining that "we are really powerless to conduct air strikes" in Bosnia, because "the United Nations has not been asking for air strikes."

What followed over the next several years was a uniquely Clintonesque brand of foreign policy liberalism. On the one hand, the president's evident discomfort with the use of American power, his preference for action in concert with and on behalf of the "world community," and his exuberant faith in the liberalizing powers of commerce and technology all traced back to a quintessentially wishful brand of idealism. "The forces of global integration are a great tide, inexorably wearing away the established order of things," Clinton exulted in 1997. In the president's telling, that "great tide" reduced a complex and dangerous world environment to a simple narrative of material progress and moral improvement, the benefits of which could already be glimpsed in a New Middle East, an African Renaissance and even a "strategic partnership" with China.

Among the detritus that "global integration" would wash away were traditional considerations of power, which members of the Clinton team derided as "yesterday's preoccupations" and "stratocrap and globaloney." In place of traditional concerns about aggression and

power, the Clintonites discerned new, more urgent threats—a catalogue of twenty-first-century perils ranging from crime syndicates to
global warming and the flu. With a grand sweep, Undersecretary of
State Strobe Talbot located national security challenges "from the
floor of the stock exchange in Singapore to the roof of the world over
Patagonia where there is a hole in the ozone layer," while Vice President Al Gore likened the struggle to contain global environmental
degradation to past American efforts against the Soviet Union.

All the while the administration was confusing these worries
with actual threats, it was ignoring the persistence of behavior that
did not accord with its worldview. "If the American people don't know
anything else about me," the president reminded the public in 1999,
"they know that I don't like to use military force." So, having apolo-
gized for the conduct of his Cold War predecessors in Africa and elsewhere, Clinton sat out the genocide in Rwanda, and for too long, the
attempted genocide in Bosnia—which, recalling Neville Chamberlain,
Secretary of State Warren Christopher infamously described as "a
humanitarian crisis a long way from home, in the middle of another
continent." The administration dithered for nearly three years while
Bosnia burned and the president visited Holocaust memorials. And
when, in 1994, North Korea's effort to produce nuclear weapons threatened to drag the United States into a war, the Clinton team permitted
Jimmy Carter to cut a deal and tried to bribe Pyongyang into aban-
doning its bid for nuclear weapons with pledges of American assistance. Echoing Carter's insistence that the upshot of his negotiations
"was kind of like a miracle," Clinton boasted, "This agreement will
help achieve a long-standing and vital American objective: an end to
the threat of nuclear proliferation on the Korean peninsula." (The
"miracle" culminated in 2002 in the announcement by North Korea
that it had not abandoned its efforts to produce nuclear weapons.)

In the meantime, just next door, the very men that candidate
Clinton had called "the butchers of Beijing" were modernizing their
armed forces and firing missiles off Taiwan, stealing and then exporting American military technology, and threatening the United States
itself. In response, President Clinton showered China with dual-use
military technology, toasted their new "strategic partnership," and
officially "delinked" human rights and trade.

The Clinton team's response to terrorism proved similarly feck-less. Despite a clear evidence trail leading back to Al Qaeda, it failed to respond to the October 2000 attack on the USS *Cole,* and vetoed proposals to dispatch Special Forces in the hunt for Osama bin Laden. In a similar vein, it never responded to the 1996 attack on the Kho-bar Towers Air Force barracks in Saudi Arabia, despite (or because of) evidence of involvement by Iran, which the Clinton team was then attempting to "engage." Then too, the administration's response to the bombing of two American embassies in East Africa in August 1998 was to fling a few missiles at a pharmaceutical plant in Sudan on the eve of Clinton's impeachment. In fact, his administration never truly responded to terrorist attacks with the long reach of American mili-tary power. Doing so was a matter for the "long reach of our nation's law enforcement," as Madeleine Albright explained. The Clinton administration even gave state sponsors of terrorism a linguistic cleans-ing, changing their official title from "rogue states" to "states of concern."

Still, Bill Clinton was no George McGovern. He might be dovish by temperament, but if the price of inaction proved politically steeper than the alternative, the president could be counted on to act. Hence, the uncontested occupation of Haiti commenced only when the prospect of boatloads of Haitians washing up on Florida's beaches, combined with protests from the Congressional Black Caucus, had backed Clinton into a corner. The president's Balkan point man, Richard Holbrooke, likewise recounts that Clinton decided to launch a sustained bombing campaign in Bosnia only after the Europeans began pressing the United States to honor a pledge to evacuate their hapless peacekeepers, a politically risky operation likely to produce substantial U.S. casualties—which air strikes would, and did, make unnecessary. Nor was the Clinton team any more eager to act in Kosovo. And when it did, with an eye to the polls, it kept attack air-craft above an altitude of 15,000 feet, ruled out the use of ground troops, and then subordinated the mission of U.S. peacekeepers to the imperative of "force protection."

This peculiar mixture of liberalism and cynicism produced its clearest failure in Iraq. According to the administration's scorecard, it was not the integrity of containment or even the value of keeping

Saddam disarmed that mattered. Far more important was the political imperative of keeping Iraq "off the President's desk," as one administration official put it. In those instances when Clinton actually located Iraq on his desk, the administration did not perform much better. Advertising their fears as if they were virtues, the Clinton team repeatedly appealed to the United Nations for help in extricating the administration from binds of its own devising. The White House abandoned members of Iraq's democratic opposition, in many cases to a gruesome fate. It presided over the dismantling of the containment apparatus that the previous administration had used to keep Saddam "in his box." And when it did resort to the use of force, the administration employed tit-for-tat military operations that had no demonstrable effect on a worsening situation. The proclaimed effectiveness of these operations was contrived and largely fanciful. The whole business reflected the administration's refusal to employ measures of genuine strategic effectiveness. The Clinton policy toward Iraq may have comforted the sensibilities of its architects—but not nearly so much as it comforted Saddam Hussein, who, by the time Clinton left office, was out of the box whose confines had been mostly imaginary to begin with.

SIX

A Distinctly American Internationalism (Bush II)

Liberals and realists approach the world from different directions, but when it comes to Iraq, both have ended up in the same place: watching Saddam's arsenal grow ever more threatening. For each ideology tends to impel America toward a minimalist approach to foreign policy—one because the very concept of self-interest provokes discomfort, and the other because it defines the national interest far too narrowly. On the question of what to do about Saddam in particular, both of these worldviews generated excuses for inaction. But on the question of Iraq, and on the broader question of how to use American power in the world, there was always an alternative. After September 11, 2001, President George W. Bush embraced it.

This alternative is what President Bush calls "a distinctly American internationalism," a philosophy that seeks to combine the most successful elements of realism and liberalism. This worldview was not created out of whole cloth by the Bush administration. Marrying American power to American ideals, presidents from Teddy Roosevelt and Harry Truman to John F. Kennedy and Ronald Reagan all put into practice the tenets of a distinctly American internationalism, and did so to great effect. On the 2000 campaign trail, Senator John McCain's call for a policy of "rogue state rollback" harkened back to this tradition, as did candidate Bush's call for a foreign policy that embraced "idealism, without illusions" and "realism, in the service of American ideals." Though he was uncertain in charting such a course during his first year in office, September 11 prompted the president to return to his campaign slogan and build on it. Bush subsequently embraced the inheritance of Truman and Kennedy, promising to "fight, for a just peace—a peace that favors liberty." This, in turn, brought him logically and quickly to the problem of Saddam Hussein.

What does "distinctly American internationalism"—or simply American internationalism—mean? First, it clearly follows from "American exceptionalism"—a belief in the uniqueness and the virtue of the American political system that, when translated into foreign policy terms, offers the United States as a model for the world. It is a model because faith in the universal ideal of freedom, not a blood-and-soil nationalism, is what defines the American idea. The historian Robert Tucker describes how this faith has shaped the contours of our foreign policy:

> From the outset of our existence as a nation we have believed that our security and survival are synonymous with the security and survival of freedom in the world. This is why our reason of state has not only had a dimension above and beyond a conventional reason, but has been regularly seen as somehow qualitatively different from it.

Contemporary liberals and realists tend to deny that America is an exceptional nation in any sense. Today's liberals are suspicious of this idea because the notion of America's uniqueness contradicts the logic of cultural relativism and encourages American nationalism. Realists believe that to concede this exceptionalism would encourage America's "crusading impulse." In the postwar era, this distinction set American internationalists like Harry Truman and John F. Kennedy apart from wishful liberals like Henry Wallace and Eleanor Roosevelt, on the one hand, and from realists like George Kennan and Henry Kissinger, on the other. Where liberals argue that peace and political liberty can best be fostered within international organizations and through international cooperation, American internationalists look to American power and American-led alliances. And while a deep-seated reluctance to judge others and lingering skepticism about America's founding ideals weigh down liberals, no such misgivings inhibit American internationalists. To be sure, some liberals concede that America should play the role of global policemen—at least in conjunction with the "world community." But for American internationalists, America's mission goes beyond so limited a view.

If this attachment to the American idea distinguishes American internationalists from liberals, it equally sets them apart from realists. When, for example, Harry Truman pledged in 1947 to "assist free peoples to work out their own destinies in their own way," realists like Walter Lippmann warned that the president had launched a dangerous crusade. American internationalists do concur with certain tenets of realism—above all, the view of the international environment as a fundamentally dangerous place. Where the two worldviews part company is precisely over the American internationalist claim that this condition may be significantly ameliorated through the vigorous application of American power and ideals.

The heyday of American internationalism—or liberal anticommunism, as it was called at the time—began with Truman's declaration that the United States had become "one of the most powerful forces for good on earth," and that the task now was to "keep it so" and to "lead the world to peace and prosperity." NSC-68, the famous statement of national security policy that Truman commissioned in 1950, insisted that "a defeat of free institutions anywhere is a defeat everywhere." American internationalism, with its faith in liberal democracy and America's duty to encourage it around the globe, was now enshrined in official policy and would remain there through the administration of John F. Kennedy, who famously vowed that the United States would "pay any price, bear any burden, meet any hardship, support any friend, oppose any foe to assure the survival and the success of liberty."

By 1968, however, this form of American internationalism was seemingly being discredited in the jungles of Southeast Asia. The war in Vietnam persuaded many liberals that not only American policy, but also the fundamental character of the United States had been tested and found wanting. The United States, as former Kennedy official Richard Barnet argued in 1971, ought to be viewed "not as the problem-solver of the world but as an integral part of the problem." Or as President Carter put it a few years later, Vietnam taught that America should not "become militarily involved in the internal affairs of another nation unless there is a direct and obvious threat to the security of the United States or its people." The lessons of Munich, which counseled resistance to aggression abroad, had been replaced by the lessons of Vietnam.

In truth, Vietnam generated not one, but two misleading lessons—one for the political left and one for the right. Some realists had warned against America's intervention in Southeast Asia from the outset, seeing it as the logical consequence of ideology run amok. The outcome only confirmed their suspicions. The lesson, then, was that America should intervene only where its "vital interests" were threatened, not on the "periphery" and never for ideological reasons. Thus, even as his administration continued to wage war in Vietnam, President Nixon proclaimed, "the objective of any American administration would be to avoid another war like Vietnam any place in the world." America would do this by looking "to the nation directly threatened to assume the primary responsibility of providing the manpower for its defense." It would also lean heavily on the European brand of *realpolitik* espoused by national security advisor Henry Kissinger, which led to strenuous efforts to improve relations with the Soviet Union and with China, even as the two powers continued to aid America's foe in Southeast Asia. The "détente" that grew out of this initiative would last the better part of a decade.

During the 1970s, then, liberalism and realism tended to act as mutually reinforcing barriers to the exercise of American power. While future Clinton aide Anthony Lake applauded a "welcome shift toward recognition of the limits of American power and responsibility," Kissinger similarly counseled "restraint in the uses of power." Yet as liberals and conservatives alike abandoned the foreign policy tenets that had guided America through the first phase of the Cold War, a small group of Democrats and Republicans held to that philosophy. In the aftermath of George McGovern's 1972 defeat, a group of American internationalists—or neoconservatives, as they would soon be called—close to Senator Henry "Scoop" Jackson formed the Coalition for a Democratic Majority (CDM), which directly challenged the isolationism that had taken control of much of the Democratic Party. Unlike his party's dovish establishment, Jackson and his colleagues at the CDM insisted that America's self-interest and the interests of mankind were not inherently incompatible. On the contrary, they claimed that the world was a better place as a result of the vigorous application of American power. Accordingly, Jackson counseled a foreign policy that was at once robust, idealistic and interventionist. In the Democratic Party of the 1970s, however, this was hardly an easy sell. Nor was it much more welcome in the Republican Party of Gerald Ford, whose devotion to *realpolitik* was considered by American internationalists almost as dangerous as the Democratic Party's self-flagellating foreign policy.

Rejecting the "lessons" of Vietnam, these American internationalists of the 1970s stood for continuity with the postwar foreign policy tradition. They remained convinced of the need for continued American vigilance abroad, particularly in dealing with the Soviet Union. It is easy to forget how controversial was the suggestion in the mid-to-late 1970s that the USSR was really a danger, much less one that should be confronted by the United States. This was hardly the dominant view of the American foreign policy establishment. Quite the contrary: Prevailing wisdom from the Nixon through the Carter administrations held that the United States should do its utmost to coexist peaceably with the USSR, and that the American people in any case were not capable of sustaining a serious challenge to the Soviet system. To engage in an arms race would either bankrupt the United States or lead to Armageddon. To challenge communist ideology at its core, to declare it evil and illegitimate, would be at best quixotic and possibly perilous. When American internationalists challenged this consensus, when they criticized détente and arms control and called for a military buildup and a broad ideological and strategic assault on Soviet communism, their recommendations were generally dismissed as either naïve or reckless. It would take a revolution in American foreign policy, the fall of the Berlin Wall and the disintegration of the Soviet empire to prove them right.

Having fallen out of favor for a decade and a half, the tradition of distinctly American internationalism was revived by President Reagan, who pledged that the decisive factor in the Cold War would "not be bombs and rockets, but a test of wills and ideas," and that the United States would help other nations "foster the infrastructure of democracy." Reagan rebuilt the United States military. He advanced the Reagan Doctrine, which took seriously the admonition to roll back Soviet gains, and did so by supporting anticommunist insurgencies around the world. He helped found quasi-governmental organizations like the National Endowment for Democracy, which encouraged political freedoms in autocratic countries. He described the Soviet Union for what it was—an evil empire. Reagan believed that only by changing the political systems of our adversaries, rather than "balancing" or "engaging" them, could we ensure a safer America and a more secure world. Most important, he spoke openly and frequently about America's mission in that world. The Reagan inheritance languished for more than a decade but then, after 9-11, George W. Bush revived it once again.

It is no small irony that the task of ousting Saddam Hussein has fallen to the son of the president who, among other things, made the fateful decision to leave Saddam in power. It is also striking that President George W. Bush quotes approvingly George Marshall's prediction that "our flag will be recognized throughout the world as a symbol of freedom on the one hand, and of overwhelming power on the other," after candidate Bush placed misgivings about military intervention at the center of his foreign policy agenda. While American internationalists saw the Clinton administration as weak and indecisive, Bush foreign policy advisor Stephen Hadley complained that it had "been too quick to reach out to the military instrument." And on the campaign trail George W. Bush flatly asserted that he would not intervene to stop "genocide in nations outside our strategic interest" and that the United States needed to adopt a more "humble" approach to the world.

Contrasting his own foreign policy, which would focus on "vital national interests," with Clinton's moralism, Bush's critiques often seemed to shade into contempt for democracy itself. "The new Pakistani general, he's just been elected—not elected, this guy took over office," Bush said of coup leader Pervez Musharraf during the infamous name-the-president-of-Pakistan ambush. "It appears this guy is going to bring stability to the country, and I think that's good news for the subcontinent." Indeed, for all his invocations of Reagan, it appeared that Bush's approach would amount to nothing more than a variation of old-world *realpolitik* and an echo of Gerald Ford. "[T]he emergent ethos," noted Jonathan Clarke, a realist at the Cato Institute, shortly after Bush took office, "is of a return to professionalism taking precedence over ideology."

Bush's choice of senior foreign policy aides only bolstered that impression. Borrowing a line of reasoning that derived partly from Hans Morgenthau and partly from *Reader's Digest,* his newly appointed secretary of state, Colin Powell, had argued in a 1992 *New York Times* op-ed that the United States should not intervene in Bosnia because the conflict has "deep ethnic and religious roots that go back a thousand years." Nor should America aid the Iraqi insurgents, lest it end up "trying to sort out two thousand years of Mesopotamian history." America, Powell had said, should act only in those instances where "the cold calculus of national interest" was at stake. In a similar vein, Bush national security advisor Condoleezza Rice came to the president's attention as a protégé of his father's close friend Brent Scowcroft and espoused an unsentimental brand of *realpolitik* identical to her mentor's. Powell chose another Scowcroft protégé, Richard Haass, as his Middle East point man and director of policy planning. In his writings Haass had advised that "order is more fundamental than justice" and, hence, "even though the world would be far better off without Saddam, making his ouster an explicit goal would also be wrong."

Bush, though, also appointed several American internationalists to prominent posts in his administration. "We need to strengthen our ties to democratic allies and to challenge regimes hostile to our interests and values," declared a statement of foreign policy principles produced by the Project for a New American Century that Secretary of Defense Donald Rumsfeld and a group of future Bush aides signed two years before Bush took office. Rumsfeld's deputy, Paul Wolfowitz, was equally committed to the role of principles in U.S. foreign policy. He came to prominence in 1976 as a member of "Team B," a group of conservative foreign policy hands whose report turned on its head the intelligence community's benign reading of Soviet strategic intentions. During the Reagan and Bush administrations, Wolfowitz quickly rose through the State Department and Pentagon ranks. In 1992 he provoked an uproar at both ends of the political spectrum when, as undersecretary for policy at the Pentagon, he urged exploiting America's military supremacy for the purpose of "deterring potential competitors from even aspiring to a larger regional or global role." Nor did he advocate this merely for geopolitical reasons. During the 1990s, Wolfowitz emerged as a tireless champion of ethnic minorities from Bosnia's Muslims to Iraq's Kurds. Writing in the *National Interest* just before taking office, Wolfowitz complained, "Nothing could be less realistic than the versions of the 'realist' view of foreign policy that dismisses human rights, an important tool of American foreign policy."

Shortly after his inauguration, Bush said of his foreign policy team, "There's going to be disagreements. I hope there is disagreement." There was—but not along familiar lines. When it came to the issue of American power, our bureaucratic actors in recent years had their lines down pat. The State Department counseled an active role on the international scene; the Pentagon, hobbled by the "lessons" of Vietnam, advised restraint. Even in the administration of Ronald Reagan, which appeared united behind a single vision, there were epic battles between Pentagon chief Caspar Weinberger and Secretary of State George Shultz, who complained that America was turning into "the Hamlet of nations, worrying endlessly over whether and how to respond" to its foes. Recall, too, Madeleine Albright's famous query to Colin Powell, chairman of the Joint Chiefs during the Clinton administration: "What's the point of having this superb military that you're always talking about if we can't use it?"

But on the question of Iraq, the Bush team has reversed the equation, pitting a State Department that warns about the perils of the use of force against a Pentagon team that believes in its efficacy. To the State Department, Colin Powell has brought his peculiar brand of realism, while to the Pentagon, robust internationalists like Rumsfeld and Wolfowitz have brought their more expansive views of America's global role. When it comes to Iraq, the disagreements between the two camps date back to the first Bush administration, when Powell successfully argued for halting the war after only four days and denying aid to Iraqi insurgents, and Wolfowitz dissented from his own administration's decision to leave Saddam Hussein in power and then spent much of the past decade lobbying for aid to the Iraqi rebels. He now recommends that the United States strike Iraq as soon as "we find the right way to do it." Rumsfeld, for his part, contends, "Iraq today is ripe for a broad-based insurrection."

Yet, having pledged to deal forcefully with Baghdad, the Bush team spent its first months in office not doing so. Like the Clinton team before it, the Bush administration declined to authorize the release of congressionally appropriated funds for use by the opposition inside Iraq. Instead, the State Department audited them. In fact, far from transforming containment into rollback, the White House proceeded to water down even the demands that the Clinton team had imposed on Iraq. Only two months after coming to office, Powell began promoting a plan to ease the decade-old sanctions regime against America's Gulf War foe. He intended the plan, which called for the elimination of most restrictions on Iraqi trade and a tightening of the embargo on military imports, "to relieve the burden on the Iraqi people" and thereby defuse criticism of the United States.

Powell headed off to the Middle East in March 2001 to sell his plan. His friends in the region, Powell said, had told him it was "the right thing to do." But Powell's friends in Washington—namely, the president, the vice president and the defense secretary—had told him nothing of the kind, as Powell acknowledged during his trip. Nor were the Iraqis buying his sales pitch: officials in Baghdad promptly termed his proposal "rubbish." Powell's Arab "friends," too, began disparaging the idea as soon as he got back on his plane. Nonetheless, the secretary of state soldiered on, pushing his plan both at home and at the United Nations. Eventually he succeeded. But when the United Nations finally signed off on Powell's new sanctions regime, it accepted the carrot and rejected the stick. While it gladly authorized easing the embargo against Iraq, the final version of its plan left out its only tough elements: commitments from Iraq's neighbors to stop illegal oil imports and to host international monitors along Iraq's borders. "This significant step will improve the Iraqi regime's ability to meet the needs of its people," Powell declared. Saddam had gotten something for nothing.

Then came September 11. That day may not have changed the views of some of the president's diplomatic counselors. It may not even have changed the threat posed by Saddam Hussein. But it did change the president, and therefore the direction of his foreign policy.

Exactly how much the president and his policies had evolved after the attack may be gleaned from a series of speeches Bush delivered between September 2001 and June 2002, as well as from the national

security strategy document in which their themes were formally enun-
ciated. In the space of less than an hour, during his address to a joint
session of Congress on September 20, 2001, Bush transformed himself from a realist following in his father's footsteps to an internationalist touting America's ideals as sincerely and forcefully as Harry
Truman, John Kennedy and Ronald Reagan before him. Bush described
America's purpose in this way:

> The advance of human freedom, the great achievement of our time
> and the great hope of every time, now depends on us. Our nation,
> this generation, will lift the dark threat of violence from our peo-
> ple and our future. We will rally the world to this cause by our efforts,
> by our courage. We will not tire, we will not falter, and we will not
> fail.

All of these things the president demonstrated in the following months
by concentrating America's military power to devastating effect in
Afghanistan. There the United States not only destroyed bin Laden's
refuge, but toppled one of the most repressive governments in the
world, thereby encouraging women to show their faces, children to
fly their kites, and men to get a shave and speak their minds for the
first time in years. President Bush, it was said, had translated "moral
clarity" into official policy.

That moral clarity was reinforced in the president's January 29
State of the Union address, when he famously identified Iraq, Iran
and North Korea as members of the "axis of evil." In the days following that speech, gasps could still be heard from Washington to New
York to every European capital. Not since Ronald Reagan described
the Soviet Union as an evil empire had an American president so
boldly flouted the foreign policy establishment's conventional wisdom and euphemistic language. The *New York Times* instantly expressed
alarm and discomfort that "the application of power and intimida-
tion has returned to the forefront of American foreign policy." For
their part, a chorus of former Clinton administration officials complained that the president had overstated the threats to America and
underestimated the perils of responding to them.

Nowhere were the complaints louder than in the case of Iraq,
where it was rapidly becoming clear that Bush would break with the

policies of his predecessors. Over the next few months, in a series of speeches and interviews, the president explained why Iraq was indeed a threat like no other, and how September 11 had demonstrated the urgent need to confront it. In a September 2002 address to the U.N. General Assembly, he detailed Saddam Hussein's aggression, his attempts to acquire and develop weapons of mass destruction, his depredations against the Iraqi people, his defiance of the U.N. itself, and finally, his support for terrorism. Elaborating on these themes in an October 7 speech in Cincinnati, Bush warned,

> While there are many dangers in the world, the threat from Iraq stands alone—because it gathers the most serious dangers of our age in one place. Iraq's weapons of mass destruction are controlled by a murderous tyrant who has already used chemical weapons to kill thousands of people. This same tyrant has tried to dominate the Middle East, has invaded and brutally occupied a small neighbor, has struck other nations without warning, and holds an unrelenting hostility toward the United States. By its past and present actions, by its technological capabilities, by the merciless nature of its regime, Iraq is unique.

September 11 did not create the threat of Saddam Hussein, or even make the imperative of dealing with the threat more urgent. Rather, it dramatized a threat that was there all along. Before that day, the president reminded Americans, "we had only hints of Al Qaeda's plans and designs." But now, in Iraq, "we see a threat whose outlines are far more clearly defined, and whose consequences could be far more deadly. . . . Understanding the threats of our time, knowing the designs and deceptions of the Iraqi regime, we have every reason to assume the worst, and we have an urgent duty to prevent the worst from occurring." Nor, as the president has made clear, will America's duty be discharged when Saddam is toppled, or even when Iraq subsequently has a decent government. The Bush Doctrine has regime change in Iraq as its focal point, but it provides guidance and a mission for American foreign policy as a whole.

Thus, on June 1, 2002, in an address at West Point, Bush elaborated on themes he had in the past applied primarily to Iraq, spelling out what would henceforth be known as the Bush Doctrine. First, he said that the United States would no longer rely solely on "Cold-War doctrines of containment and deterrence." Instead, it would reserve the right to preempt threats, to "take the battle to the enemy, disrupt his plans, and confront the worst threats before they emerge." Second, the United States would actively promote its principles abroad, recognizing that "the requirements of freedom apply fully to Africa and Latin American and the entire Islamic world." Finally, the United States would do what was necessary to remain the world's sole super-power, or as the president put it, "America has, and intends to keep, military strengths beyond challenge, thereby making the destabilizing arms races of other eras pointless, and limiting rivalries to trade and other pursuits of peace." Thus, just as the particular events of the late 1940s yielded the broad commitment that guided America through the Cold War, so have September 11 and the threat from Iraq combined to produce a national security doctrine that responds to the broader dangers of the new century. The Bush Doctrine articulates an affirmative vision of American leadership, one that is neither reactive to nor dependent on the emergence of a specific threat.

In late September 2002, the White House published "The National Security Strategy of the United States," a document that codified the three principles President Bush had spelled out at West Point: preemption, regime change and American leadership. The publication of this document inaugurated a new era, a shift in perception about America's global role comparable to the advent of the containment doctrine a half-century earlier. It transformed the war from a police action to round up the perpetrators of September 11 into a campaign to uproot tyranny and export democracy. It also transformed the tenets of a distinctly American internationalism into the official policy of the U.S. government.

The Bush national security strategy bears little resemblance to strategy documents produced by the Clinton administration or, for that matter, by Bush's father. Harry Truman or Ronald Reagan, on the other hand, would have found this robust approach to the international scene familiar. The Bush document speaks bluntly about the imperative of American leadership, stating that we must "dissuade potential adversaries from pursuing a military build-up in hopes of surpassing, or equaling, the power of the United States." At the same time, it defends American primacy on moral grounds:

> In keeping with our heritage and principles, we do not use our strength to press for unilateral advantage. We seek instead to create a balance of power that favors human freedom: conditions in which all nations and all societies can choose for themselves the rewards and challenges of political and economic liberty. By making the world safer, we allow the people of the world to make their own lives better.

Yet if the Bush Doctrine is unequivocal in its commitment to promoting democracy, it is also grounded in the reality of self-interest. "To forestall or prevent ... hostile acts from our adversaries," it adds, "the United States will, if necessary, act preemptively." There is no contradiction here. The emphasis on preemption derives from the recognition that the world has grown too small and too dangerous to allow, in some instances, the luxury of mere containment. And preemption against dictators developing weapons of mass destruction clearly serves the interest of democracies. The national security strategy seeks to minimize the gap between ideals and interests, between morality and power. It gathers in one place all the major strands of a distinctly American internationalism.

America's Mission

SEVEN

From Deterrence to Preemption

T he first element of the Bush Doctrine is a willingness to acknowledge that under certain circumstances, preemptive action will be required. Deterrence and containment, according to the new National Security Strategy, no longer suffice: "Given the goals of rogue states and terrorists, the United States can no longer rely on a reactive posture as we have in the past." Instead, America must identify and destroy the threat posed by those who would do us harm "before it reaches our borders." Why? Because of what President Bush at West Point described as a world standing at "the crossroads of radicalism and technology," where "weak states and small groups could attain a catastrophic power to strike great nations." Those crossroads meet most clearly in Iraq.

Some critics of the Bush Doctrine argue that containment—resting ultimately on deterrence—is a more measured alternative to preemption. Iraq is contained in a geopolitical "box," these critics argue, so why run the risk of preemption and war? Before examining this argument, we would do well to cast a glance backward, for this is hardly the first time we have heard the argument. Prior to Operation Desert Storm, the claim that containment would defang Saddam was a commonplace among many in the Democratic Party. In 1990, Senator Tom Harkin expressed surprise that "there are some even today who say that Saddam has already won. Quite to the contrary, he is losing every day.... Do we want to wait a year and a half, perhaps, for sanctions to really have their effect, or to perhaps lose 20,000 American lives in a war that would take place early this year?" Echoing this assessment, former Carter national security advisor Zbigniew Brzezinski said, "we should stay on course applying the policy of punitive containment. This policy is working. Iraq has been deterred, ostracized and punished." Today, Madeleine Albright insists that U.N. resolutions "keep Iraq in its box," while Senator Carl Levin claims, "Containment is so far working." Not to be outdone, Jimmy Carter assures us that "there is no current danger to the United States from Baghdad."

The question is, having been so wrong before, are the liberal proponents of containment any more right now? Hardly. The notion that "containment is working" is wishful. Whereas in 1999, Iraq smuggled only about $350 million worth of oil out of the country, today Saddam accrues about $3 billion a year in illicit oil exports. To Syria alone, Baghdad is smuggling something like 200,000 barrels of oil per day. It is also skimming money from the U.N.'s oil-for-food program, requiring surcharges for every barrel of oil sold, which has netted it hundreds of millions of dollars. Commercial airliners routinely flout the embargo against Iraq; country after country has resumed diplomatic relations with Baghdad; Chinese, Russian and French firms have raced to sign contracts with Saddam; and Arab leaders, from former foes like Saudi Arabia and Egypt to the members of the Arab League, have warmly re-embraced him.

The Iraqi military, too, has improved its fortunes—acquiring spare parts and other prohibited items from countries like China and Serbia; improving its ability to target allied aircraft; challenging American warplanes on a regular basis; and periodically making feints toward the Kuwaiti border. More important, according to former weapons inspectors, Western intelligence agencies and defectors, Saddam has kept alive his program to develop weapons of mass destruction. Noting that as many as twenty Scud missiles remain unaccounted for, former chief weapons inspector Richard Butler warns that Iraq "remains at work" on its WMD program, and that "containment is not the answer." The former head of Iraq's nuclear programs, Khidir Hamza, adds that the window of opportunity to halt Saddam's WMD efforts "is closing down possibly within the next 2–3 years." Vice President Cheney summarizes the case of those who insist that containment is working: "The argument comes down to this: Yes, Saddam is as dangerous as we say he is. We just need to let him get stronger before we do anything about it."

There are two possible futures. One of them, says former weapons inspector Charles Duelfer, "is an Iraq carried forward under this regime with the potential of weapons of mass destruction, with leverage of four or five million barrels a day of oil production, with its track record, with its pattern of aggression, with its pattern of dominating not just its own people but its neighbors." The other alternative, Duelfer continues, "is a positive Iraq, an Iraq under a government that behaves more by international norms" and which could be "the engine of development in the Middle East." That second alternative, needless to say, is impossible so long as Saddam rules over Iraq.

Of course, not all of the opposition to invading Iraq comes from the left. In the fall of 2002, several prominent officials who had served George Herbert Walker Bush took to the op-ed pages and airwaves in full cry against military action. For the most part, their arguments were based on deterrence—the idea that America's vast arsenal could keep Saddam from ever resorting to his own. "Threatening to use [his] weapons for blackmail—much less their actual use," Brent Scowcroft wrote in the *Wall Street Journal*, "would open him and his entire regime to a devastating response by the U.S. While Saddam is thoroughly evil, he is above all a power-hungry survivor." Or as conservative columnist Steve Chapman argued, "We don't have to wonder if he can be deterred from using weapons of mass destruction. He already has been."

The realist argument for deterrence is weak. The logic of deterrence—specifically, the threat of massive retaliation—functioned as intended during the Cold War. Then, the absolute certainty that the United States and the Soviet Union could destroy one another at the push of a button finally prevented either from doing so. The entire framework, however, always depended on the assumption that Soviet leaders were fundamentally rational actors, and conservative ones at that. And, indeed, however brutal they may have been, Khrushchev, Brezhnev and Gorbachev did not wish to see their country laid waste in a nuclear exchange. Can deterrence, depending as it does on an adversary who maintains some semblance of sanity, work with Saddam?

The fact is that Saddam has revealed himself to be a pathological risk-taker. Theories of deterrence notwithstanding, he attacked Iran under the misguided belief that its regime would quickly collapse; attacked Israel under the mistaken assumption that doing so would collapse Arab support for the American-led coalition; and attacked Kuwait because he calculated that the United States would not respond. Equally important, he lives in a vacuum, depending on information from yes-men who share his delusions. The U.S. Air Force's official study of Desert Storm, *The Gulf War Air Power Survey,* described his calculations this way: "Iraqi arrogance—which afflicted both Saddam and his generals—and which manifested itself in a predisposition to inflate Iraqi capabilities and underestimate those of their enemies, had a significant impact on his assessment of the balance of forces."

Further clouding his ability to see clearly is his faith in soothsayers, who informed his every move during the Gulf War, his lack of credible information about U.S. intentions, his track record of heedless risk-taking, and most of all, his supreme irrationality. "If we cannot fully understand the acts of other people, until we think we know what they know," Walter Lippmann once observed, "then in order to do justice we have to appraise not only the information which has been at their disposal, but the minds through which they have filtered it." To deter Saddam effectively, then, we must understand the mind through which he filters his information. As an effective framework for deterrence, that is a shaky foundation indeed.

Brent Scowcroft may think that Saddam will never employ his deadly arsenal. But before we send the former national security advisor to hammer out an arms control agreement with Saddam, Scowcroft needs to explain much more convincingly how weapons of mass destruction transform Third World dictators into rational-choice theorists. Writing of "the 'psychological' element in deterrence, on which all else depends," Jonathan Schell, dean of nuclear abolitionists, notes that a leader's "state of mind—his self-interest, his sanity, his prudence, his self-control, his clear-sightedness—is the real foundation of his country's and everyone else's survival. In short, he must decide that the world he lives in is not one in which aggression pays off." Sanity, prudence and self-control, needless to say, are not the first qualities that leap to mind when you think of Saddam Hussein.

In any case, it makes perfect sense for Saddam to amass a vast arsenal if his aim is to dominate his region and deter the United States.

Today we may attack Iraq with minimal risk because Saddam has yet to acquire a nuclear bomb. Once he does, the equation changes. Then it is we who will be deterred. For evidence of this proposition, we need look no further than North Korea. In the aftermath of that country's announcement that it did indeed possess nuclear material, the *Washington Post*'s Mary McGrory wondered "why it is necessary for us to bomb, invade and occupy Iraq while North Korea gets the striped-pants treatment." The answer is obvious: Iraq does not yet have the bomb. If and when it does, it will, like North Korea, acquire the ability to "blackmail" or deter the United States, and also will get "striped-pants treatment." Thus, Iraq's drive to build a bomb is entirely logical. Armed with nuclear weapons, a rational Saddam could just as easily deter us from responding to his provocations as an irrational Saddam. He could then commit aggression or engage in regional blackmail and believe that the United States—fearing loss of lives by its allies or even by itself—would be deterred from acting against him. Hence, the unpalatable choice offered by advocates of deterrence: Assume Saddam is a madman and wait until he assembles the tools of aggression, or assume he is rational and wait until he assembles the tools of aggression.

What foreign policy analysts wedded to the old verities about deterrence seem to forget is that the world has changed since the Cold War, and along with it the nature of the threats facing the United States. Aside from the death of Soviet communism, the main thing that has changed is that more countries possess weapons of mass destruction and means to deliver them. In the past few years alone, India and Pakistan have set off a combined total of twelve atomic explosions; Pakistan, Iran, North Korea and China have test-launched ballistic missiles; Iraq, Syria and Libya have ongoing missile programs; and China, Russia and North Korea have continued to export ballistic missile technology throughout the Middle East. U.S. policymakers have been slow to recognize the danger. As late as 1998, Joint Chiefs chairman Henry Shelton averred that "the intelligence community can provide the necessary warning" if one of these countries is developing "an ICBM threat to the United States." But just a week after Shelton's pronouncement—and with no warning whatsoever from the intelligence community—North Korea demonstrated its intercontinental ballistic missile capability by launching a three-stage rocket over Japan. Intelligence analysts promptly dropped their nonchalance. "The probability that a missile armed with weapons of mass destruction would be used against U.S. forces or interests," a CIA-sponsored study asserted in 2000, "is higher today than during most of the Cold War and will continue to grow."

Not all of these countries, of course, are ruled by unstable tyrants like Saddam Hussein. Indeed, the problem with deterrence calculations in an era of proliferation derives less from the nature of a given regime than from the nature of proliferation itself. If deterrence, as Henry Kissinger has written, was "barely plausible when there was only one nuclear opponent," it is certainly less so today. That is because, in an era of proliferation, the numbers have become much less favorable to the United States. Instead of betting that one adversary will think reasonably, we are now pinning our survival on the hope that six or seven will. And that figure accounts only for adversaries with return addresses. Many of America's most dangerous foes are, like Al Qaeda, nonstate actors. Because these shadowy terror networks have no home, it is virtually impossible to deter them. And it is also virtually impossible to deter states that would use terrorist groups as "cutouts" to deliver weapons. All of this is to say nothing of the questionable morality of voluntarily embracing a doctrine of mutual destruction, in which we place our civilians, and those of hostile regimes, at risk of annihilation. In any case, as September 11 should have taught us, many of our adversaries are bent on suicide and thus, by definition, are undeterrable.

If containment and deterrence no longer suffice, then America clearly needs a new roadmap. Where containment and deterrence fail—as with sociopathic dictators like Saddam and terror groups like Al Qaeda—an obvious way for the United States to safeguard its citizens is through preemption. Unfortunately, much of the debate swirling around the concept has obscured more than it has clarified. To begin with, preemption is not a novel aspect of U.S. strategy. On the contrary, the threat and possibility of preemption have been a part of American strategy for over a century. Further, its meaning is simple and clear. Preemption means striking first. And, as President Bush has explained repeatedly, avoiding another September 11 may, on rare occasions, require the United States to do exactly that. But only rarely. Lost in the media swirl over preemption is the fact that it occupies a limited place in the Bush national security strategy. The administration has emphasized repeatedly that preemption applies only "in a small number of cases" where, as Colin Powell says, "there is a threat that doesn't respond the way older threats did."

The president's critics argue that by elevating preemption from an unspoken possibility to an official policy, the president violates both the precepts of international law and decades of American military strategy. "Preemption . . . runs completely against U.S. political and strategic culture," defense expert Frank Hoffman wrote last year in an essay published by the left-leaning Center for Defense Information. For his part, former House Republican majority leader Dick Armey says preemption "would not be consistent with what we have been as a nation or what we should be as a nation." Not only that, but according to Al Gore, "What this doctrine does it to destroy the goal of a world in which states consider themselves subject to law."

But these critics of the Bush Doctrine have things backward. In international law, in international practice and in American history, there is ample precedent for the doctrine of preemption. Whether the term is "preventive attack," "anticipatory self-defense" or simply "preemption," nations have employed some form of this practice for centuries. The origins of this concept date back to the father of international law, Hugo Grotius, who in the seventeenth century wrote, "It be lawful to kill him who is preparing to kill." In a similar vein, Thomas More asserted, "If any foreign prince takes up arms and prepares to invade their land, they immediately attack him in full force outside their own borders." In America, the legitimacy of preemption was defended by Secretary of State Elihu Root, a founder of the American Society of International Law, who proclaimed in 1914 "the right of every sovereign state to protect itself by preventing a condition of affairs in which it will be too late to protect itself."

Today, indeed, the legal basis for preemption has become so broad that it permits acts of anticipatory self-defense well before an attack becomes imminent. As the political scientist Richard Regan puts it in his book *Just War,*

> Nor need a would-be victim nation wait until a would-be aggressor
> nation is immediately poised to attack before the would-be victim
> nation has just cause to strike preemptively against the would-be
> aggressor. . . . Nor need a would-be victim nation wait until a would-
> be aggressor nation has stockpiled nuclear or chemical weapons
> before the potential victim nation has just cause to strike plants
> producing such weapons of destruction.

As applied to Iraq, the United States need not even invoke a claim of
preemption. After all, by attacking Iraq it would merely be enforcing
a stack of already existing U.N. resolutions that Saddam has ignored
or violated. In this sense, an invasion of Iraq would do more to sustain international law than to erode it.

Of course, an important measure of international law is the
record of actual state practice. And since the U.N. Charter was adopted,
numerous states have practiced preemption. Not the least of these
has been the United States. One case in particular has in recent months
drawn the attention of numerous commentators and reportedly the
president. During the Cuban missile crisis of 1962, President John F.
Kennedy seriously contemplated using air strikes to destroy missile
sites erected in Cuba by the Soviets. Recognizing that weapons of
mass destruction had blurred the distinction between immediate and
looming threats, Kennedy said,

> We no longer live in a world where only the actual firing of weapons
> represents a sufficient challenge to a nation's security to constitute
> maximum peril. Nuclear weapons are so destructive and ballistic
> missiles are so swift that any substantially increased possibility of
> their use or any sudden change in their deployment may well be
> regarded as a definite threat to peace.

In this respect, Bush's emphasis on the new danger posed by the intersection of radicalism and technology echoes Kennedy forty years
before. The danger requires a greater willingness to consider preemption against one's enemies. As Henry Kissinger has put it, in the twenty-
first century, "Potential victims cannot wait until the threat has been
implemented. Preemption is inherent in the technology and ideology of the 21st century system."

Forty years ago, following extensive debate among his advisors, the president rejected advice to strike Castro. But he did engage in another form of preemption: a military blockade of Cuba to prevent the actual delivery of the Soviet missiles. While those missiles surely would have threatened the United States, they did not present a threat of imminent attack. Nonetheless, the United States acted to preempt their activation. Two decades later, in Grenada and Panama, Washington went further under the authority of preemption. In the first case, President Reagan cited the safety of American medical students in Grenada to justify the subsequent U.S. invasion; but he also made clear that his primary aim was to rid the island of growing Soviet influence. In a similar vein, President Bush justified the 1989 U.S. invasion of Panama as a response to threats against American lives and property; but administration officials openly conceded that the true aim was to prevent an unstable dictator from seizing control of the Panama Canal.

Oddly enough, given the animus toward the Bush Doctrine, it was the Clinton administration that first drew the link between the proliferation of weapons of mass destruction and the need to take preemptive action against them. In December 1993, Defense Secretary Les Aspin launched a counterproliferation program that included initiatives to prevent WMD attacks by, among other things, developing preemptive weapons that could penetrate underground bunkers to destroy chemical and biological arsenals. Less than a year later, Aspin's successor, William Perry, threatened preemptive action to destroy North Korea's growing nuclear capability. In casting preemption as a form of self-defense, both of these attempts to eliminate emerging WMD arsenals anticipated the Bush Doctrine. But the Clinton team took preemption a step further.

"Preemption as intervention, as perhaps we should have [had] in the case of Rwanda or Kosovo, is when the threat to the United States or our allies is not imminent," strategist Robert Killebrew claims. "The more serious cases involve preemption as protection, when a Saddam Hussein gets his hand on an arsenal of missiles that deliver WMD at regional or intercontinental range." A distinction between acts to preempt imminent threats and acts to preempt less imminent ones is important. In places like Haiti, Bosnia and Kosovo, the Clinton administration used force to preempt harm to those nations' citizens and their neighbors when there was no direct threat to the United States. The Democratic Party even enshrined a version of this kind of preemptive intervention in its 2000 platform. "Forward engagement," it declared, "means addressing problems early in their development before they become crises, addressing them as close to the source of the problem as possible, and having the forces and the resources to deal with these threats as soon after their emergence as possible." By the end of the 1990s, U.N. Secretary General Kofi Annan could look back and applaud "the developing norm in favour of intervention to protect civilians from wholesale slaughter."

So in important ways, the Bush administration is following in the footsteps of its predecessor. "What you are seeing in this administration is the emergence of a new principle or body of ideas . . . about what you might call the limits of sovereignty," Bush official Richard Haass said in an interview with the *New Yorker*.

> Sovereignty entails obligations. One is not to massacre your own people. Another is not to support terrorism in any way. If a government fails to meet these obligations, then it forfeits some of the normal advantages of sovereignty, including the right to be left alone inside your own territory. Other governments, including the United States, gain the right to intervene.

Outside the United States, too, preemption is a well-known tool. Perhaps the most famous—and successful—example of its use occurred in 1981, when the Israeli air force struck Iraq's Osirak nuclear plant. This operation, needless to say, was not authorized by the United Nations. In fact, the U.N., along with the United States and Great Britain, condemned it. "Israel's sneak attack on a French-built nuclear reactor near Baghdad was an act of inexcusable and short-sighted aggression," declared the *New York Times*. That, of course, did not make the Israeli strike any less wise or just. Had Israel not destroyed the reactor, Saddam would have had a nuclear capability well before the Gulf War—a fact recognized by, among others, Vice President Dick Cheney, who thanked Israel in the aftermath of that war, and today hails the strike as a template for American action. The Israeli announcement of the raid described its purpose simply: "We under no circumstances will allow an enemy to develop against our people weapons of mass destruction." The rationale, in other words, was identical to the one currently employed by the United States. "History's judgment should inform our own judgment today," says former Israeli prime minister Benjamin Netanyahu. "Did Israel launch that preemptive strike because Saddam had committed a specific act of terror against us? Did we coordinate our actions with the international community? Did we condition that operation on the approval of the United Nations? No, Israel acted alone because we understood that a nuclear-armed Saddam Hussein would place our very survival at risk." Osirak, indeed, stands as the very model for preemptive action, undertaken in the face of a clear, though hardly imminent, threat and despite howls of international protest.

O ne of the virtues of preemptive action, then, is that it is often less costly than the alternative. "History is littered with cases of inaction that led to very grave consequences for the world," Condoleezza Rice has said. "We just have to look back and ask how many dictators who ended up being a tremendous global threat and killing thousands and, indeed, millions of people, should we have stopped in their tracks." But for many, preemption remains taboo. It is primarily a unilateral tactic, and for some liberals, that itself disqualifies it as a foreign policy tool. "I believe any action in Iraq at this time, without allied support, without United Nations support . . . ," Senator Dianne Feinstein says, "would be both morally wrong and politically mistaken." Senate majority leader Tom Daschle cautions that unilateral action, which he says he would never support, could have "very, very dire consequences." In buttressing their case against such action, liberals can point to the sentiments of the international community. From the Arab world, Jordan's King Abdullah says, "In all the years I have seen in the international community, everybody is saying this is a bad idea." Staking out his own country's opposition, Germany's Gerhard Schroeder pledges flatly that "Germany will not participate" in U.S.-led military action against Iraq because "we need more peace, not more war." In Canada, Prime Minister Jean Chretien also sees no particular need to follow America's lead. Instead, "we have to follow the United Nations."

In a narrow sense, the advocates of multilateral action have a point. The United States should prefer to act in concert with other states. Doing so would not only confer broader legitimacy upon America's war aims, but also make those aims much easier to achieve—if not militarily, at least financially and politically. But must multilateral approval be the precondition for American action? Should the United States never act unilaterally?

In this instance the demand may prove unnecessary. President Bush sought and received United Nations approval—in the form of a unanimous Security Council vote—for a renewed campaign to disarm Saddam. Moreover, the Iraqi dictator is already in defiance of an entire catalogue of U.N. resolutions, which provide the United States with more than enough legal basis for punitive action. But even had the U.N. declined to lend its initial imprimatur to Bush's policy, and even if it fails to do so if and when the United States returns to the Security Council, Bush would hardly be acting without precedent if he acted unilaterally against Saddam. After all, President Clinton resorted to force without U.N. approval on several occasions, each time receiving the support of Daschle and his fellow Democrats. In 1998, for instance, France and Russia refused to allow the U.N. Security Council to authorize military action against Iraq in response to its obstruction of weapons inspections, so the United States acted without new U.N. authorization. Nor was the United States deterred when, the following year, the Security Council refused to support a resolution calling for action to halt Serb depredations in Kosovo. In the Balkans, America "faced a simple choice," recalls Clinton's Kosovo point man, Richard Holbrooke: "Act without the Security Council, or don't act at all." Again, the United States chose action over inaction.

The reason it did so was simple. The U.N. secretary general at the time, Boutros Boutros-Ghali, had things exactly wrong when he predicted a decade ago that the United Nations "may emerge as greater than the sum of its parts." Alas, whether standing by impassively during the mass slaughters in Bosnia and Rwanda or quietly tolerating Saddam's flouting of its own resolutions, the U.N. has emerged as considerably less than the sum of its parts. Or as one of Britain's former ambassadors to the U.N. put it, "There is nothing wrong with the Charter, only with the members."

It is exceedingly strange to view the United Nations as a higher moral authority than the United States. The U.N., after all, is simply a collection of sovereign states. The organization makes no distinctions based on political systems; a tyranny is as welcome as a democracy. And rather than being transformed by the U.N., these tyrannies have nearly transformed it—into an arena to pursue their agendas and propagandize their grievances. Moreover, in matters of war and peace, the only members of the United Nations that count are those who sit on the Security Council. Among its permanent members—China, Russia, Britain, the United States and France—only three qualify as mature democracies. And even they use the U.N. for their own geopolitical ends. In the case of France, for example, those ends often involve little more than obstructing the United States, an exercise often involving hypocrisy as well as malice. "In fact, even as [Prime Minister] Chirac was proclaiming the sanctity of the United Nations' authority over war-making," the *Washington Post* noted during the recent debate over weapons inspections, "some 1,000 French troops were intervening unilaterally to protect French interests in Ivory Coast."

That is doubly the case with respect to Iraq, where different countries have their own reasons for being less than resolute in the face of evil. "France and Russia have turned the United Nations into a stage from which to pursue naked self-interest," notes *Newsweek*'s Fareed Zakaria. "They have used multilateralism as a way to further unilateral policies." Russia, which according to the deputy minister of foreign affairs, Alexander Saltanov, has signed billions of dollars of contracts with Iraq in recent years, has a longstanding pecuniary interest in Saddam's well-being. China, which has complained repeatedly of America's violations of Iraqi sovereignty, has clung for years (as it did in Kosovo) to the self-serving argument that a nation should be able to do as it pleases within its own borders. The Arab states, whose Arab League warned that U.S. action against Iraq would "open the gates of hell in the Middle East," fear the popular anger a military strike could unleash—and fear even more that it might be turned against the other governments of the region, not one of which qualifies as a democracy. As for the Europeans, who furnished a good portion of Saddam's deadly inventory (France supplying nuclear technology, Germany supplying chemical agents), they seem more eager to deflate what the French like to call America's "hyperpower" than to confront Iraq's evil.

When Europeans insist that the United States defer to the consensus of the "world community," they are practicing a form of power politics dressed up as international morality. It is only at the United Nations that they can wield the influence they once wielded as individual nations. An American attack on Iraq, needless to say, diminishes that power. But instead of merely carping about American "hegemony," the Europeans could boost their defense budgets and take an active hand in insuring world stability. Instead, they spend on social programs and allow the United States to guarantee their security, and then condemn their American cousin for being too aggressive.

The obsession with building an international consensus for action against Iraq also confuses means and ends. A coalition so broad that its effect is to hamper the United States from carrying out this mission is not a coalition worth having. Because different countries bring different sensitivities and demands to multilateral undertakings, the broader the coalition becomes, the narrower America's freedom to maneuver. And for what would we be sacrificing that freedom? So France can continue to do business with Saddam? So the debt that Saddam has rung up with the Russians will be paid? Because the Saudis fear the emergence of a democracy on their border? So that Syria and other dictatorships can veto American action?

A decade ago, the first Bush administration assembled a multilateral coalition to go to war against Iraq. But it did so armed with a unilateral determination to act, with or without a "coalition of the willing" at America's side. Contrast this with President Clinton's feeble 1993 attempt to assemble a coalition for action in Bosnia. Rather than lead, Clinton permitted himself to be led—dispatching Warren Christopher to "consult" with America's European allies. When those allies refused their support, Clinton opted to avert his gaze as the slaughter in the Balkans continued.

To the most committed advocates of multilateralism, however, such drawbacks are precisely the point. Their preference for multilateralism responds to multiple needs, but most of them have nothing to do with national security. Invoking the authority of organizations like the U.N. comforts the sensibilities of those who have distaste for things military but find themselves wanting to "do something." It testifies to their virtue and good intentions. It offers assurance that U.S. military power, of which they remain suspicious, serves not only a national interest but the interests of all humanity. Best of all, from this point of view, multilateralism can inhibit the use of that power, which, in the case of Iraq, many liberals seem determined to do.

Many on the left have made the calculation that between Saddam Hussein's Iraq and George Bush's America, the latter presents the greater threat to world order. Not a few liberals have made the mistake of, in Salman Rushdie's words, "being so eager to oppose Bush that they end up seeming to back Saddam Hussein." The impulse is nothing new. During the war in Kosovo, the liberal writer David Rieff denounced "the utopian nihilism of a left that would prefer to see genocide in Bosnia and the mass deportation of the Kosovars rather than strengthen, however marginally, the hegemony of the United States." Where all this heads has been described well by essayist Christopher Hitchens: "Instead of internationalism, we find among the left now a sort of affectless, neutralist, smirking isolationism."

If the goal is to subordinate American power to the inhibitions of global consensus, U.N.-sanctioned multilateralism in theory produces isolationism in practice. Unlike the homegrown isolationists of the 1930s, who argued that America was too good for the world, the multilateralists of today argue in effect that the world is too good for America, and that only through the entanglements of a web of international constraints can America's destructive impulses be contained. Harvard professor Stanley Hoffman, for example, recommends that in Iraq's case a coalition would be "a constructive source of restraint." Summarizing the logic of Hoffman's argument, columnist Charles Krauthammer notes that "multilateralism is the isolationism of the internationalist." The impulse owes entirely to the lingering suspicion that American self-interest and the interests of humanity are inherently incompatible.

For such critics, action in concert with, and on behalf of, the international community—or strictly in self-defense, as in Afghanistan—passes the virtue test. But action against Iraq fits none of these criteria. "The crucial difference between the Democratic establishment's support for interventions in Kosovo and Bosnia," elaborates the internationalist Democrat Will Marshall, "was that they were cloaked in disinterestedness, whereas in Iraq, America's interests are directly threatened." And that, for many, makes intervention impossible. Anthony Lewis, Michael Walzer and other writers who oppose the use of force against Iraq vocally supported U.S. efforts in Kosovo because, as Walzer approvingly observed, "obviously, U.S. national security is not at stake." And where many on the right declined to support the air campaign in the Balkans because they (wrongly) failed to discern a national interest, the endorsement of liberal Democrats was based precisely on what they claimed to be the absence of such an interest.

There is, of course, a powerful moral and humanitarian argument for regime change in Iraq. But you can read all of the arguments against an invasion put forward by liberals who once could be relied on to offer moral arguments, and only seldom will you find any mention of this. The irony is that what passes for heightened moral awareness among opponents of action on the left (and right) actually amounts to moral evasion. After all, there is nothing reactionary about wanting to rid the world of a dictator who gasses his own people, invades his neighbors, develops weapons of mass destruction, and flouts an entire catalogue of U.N. resolutions. As the *New Republic* has editorialized, "the important question is not whether other countries agree with the United States but whether those countries are right." In the case of Iraq, they are not.

EIGHT

From Containment to Regime Change

The second tenet of the Bush Doctrine is regime change—that is, the recognition that the United States cannot really coexist peacefully with governments that seek to develop weapons of mass destruction, threaten their neighbors and brutalize their own citizens. The Bush Doctrine reserves the right to bring about—whether through diplomatic or military means—the demise of these regimes.

As in the case of preemption, critics of regime change denounce the tactic as evidence of "unilateralism," "imperialism" and "hubris." But is it really so wrong to topple nuclear-armed despots? The answer depends substantially on what comes next. Here the Bush Doctrine is specific: the ultimate goal of regime change is liberal democracy. Thus, the national security strategy commits the United States to "champion the cause of human dignity and oppose those who resist it" by creating "a balance of power that favors human freedom: conditions in which all nations and all societies can choose for themselves the rewards and challenges of political and economic liberty." Achieving liberal democracy in Iraq is a principal objective of the Bush administration's campaign against Saddam. "Liberty for the Iraqi people is a great moral cause, and a great strategic goal," the president said in his Cincinnati address. Why a strategic goal? "Free societies do not intimidate through cruelty and conquest," Bush explained, "and open societies do not threaten the world with mass murder." The assertion is more than a turn of phrase. It is a fact.

Of course, very few opinion makers explicitly defend Saddam Hussein, or even question the desirability of regime change in Iraq. But skeptics do challenge the feasibility of removing Saddam.

Borrowing a page from the pre–Desert Storm script, some of Bush's critics—in this case, mostly narrow realists—have revived the notion that war will "destabilize" Iraq and possibly the entire region. Thus, Colin Powell's warning of a decade ago—"It would not contribute to the stability we want in the Middle East to have Iraq fragmented into separate Sunni, Shia, and Kurd political entities"—has once more returned to favor. Better to keep Iraq together than to confront instability, the argument goes, even if the only glue available happens to be Saddam Hussein. Brent Scowcroft warns that in the event of an invasion, "Dire consequences would be the effect in the region." Among these would be "an explosion of outrage against us" and a threat to "stability and security in a vital region of the world." Scowcroft's colleague in the first Bush administration, Lawrence Eagleburger, warns similarly that the United States will become entangled in a "morass" and wonders "how we are going to deal with all of the consequences that come thereafter." Iraq's uncertain future, as opposed to its totalitarian present, has become the principle concern of many realists. "What comes after a military invasion?" Senator Chuck Hagel would like to know. "Who rules Iraq? Does the United States really want to be in Baghdad, trying to police Baghdad for twenty or thirty years?"

Behind this hand-wringing lurks a narrow *realpolitik*, brought to us by the same Metternichs who, in the name of "stability," insisted that we not upset the Iraqi order a decade ago. For realists like Scowcroft, the preference for order over liberty—whether in the Soviet Union, China or Yugoslavia—is nothing new. But the tendency to confuse international stability with the longevity of anti-American dictatorships finds its purest expression in Iraq. Yet is it really necessary to point out that Saddam's Iraq is not the Concert of Europe? Saddam's regime is a vicious dictatorship that, through aggression abroad and persecution at home, has brought to the region exactly the instability Scowcroft and others profess to fear. We have long ago passed the threshold where the prospect of, say, a fragmented Iraq is a greater evil than the persistence of Saddam Hussein. That things might be worse without him is of course a possibility. But given the status quo in Iraq, it is difficult to imagine how. To uphold the stability of a government whose demise Iraqis might be expected to cheer defies logic. Especially when, far from destabilizing the region, the replacement of Saddam Hussein would, over time, allow for greater stability.

Nevertheless, Powell and others have argued that if the United States alienates central Iraq's Sunnis, say, by overthrowing Saddam, Iraq could be plunged into chaos. (During the war in Afghanistan, Powell made the same point—wrongly, as it turned out—about over-throwing the ethnic Pashtuns who led the Taliban.) But predictions of ethnic turmoil in Iraq are even more questionable than they were in the case of Afghanistan. Unlike the Taliban, Saddam has little sup-port among any ethnic group, Sunnis included, and the Iraqi oppo-sition is itself a multiethnic force. What has brought the Kurds and Shiites to the point of open revolt is not so much disenchantment with the idea of an Iraqi nation as the simple fact that the present Iraqi government has slaughtered hundreds of thousands of them. Iraq was a multiethnic, multisectarian state before Saddam came to power, and as Iraq scholar Phebe Marr points out, "the overwhelm-ing majority of the population, except possibly for a few Kurds, has consistently shown a strong desire to keep the state together and profit from its ample resources." Echoing that assessment, the executive director of the Iraq Foundation, Rend Rahim Francke, says, "we will not have a civil war in Iraq. This is contrary to Iraqi history, and Iraq has not had a history of communal conflict as there has been in the Balkans or in Afghanistan.... Iraq will not fall apart and will not be dismembered. The Kurds have spared no words or effort in explain-ing and stressing they want to remain part of Iraq. The Shi'ia, far from wishing to secede, see themselves as quintessential Iraqi patriots."

If anything, one could argue that the aim of Iraqi unity may run counter to the aim of Iraqi stability. "One way to reconcile territorial integrity with political stability," recommends Johns Hopkins Uni-versity's Michael Mandelbaum, "is with [a] commitment to the post-war decentralization of governmental authority." Or, more precisely, make Iraq a federation. The concept is hardly without precedent in Iraqi history. Prior to Baghdad's independence from Britain, leading Iraqis endorsed the idea. A central government in Baghdad would still control most of the levers of Iraqi power, but each ethnic community would be granted limited powers of self-government—and certainly the freedom to speak their languages, celebrate their customs and practice their religious beliefs.

More important than how exactly a post-Saddam Iraq would be configured is the commitment of the United States to play a major role in the country. The task will be made considerably easier by Iraq's vast oil reserves. The moment that oil begins flowing again, the burden of rebuilding Iraq's economy will lighten considerably. Moreover, the Gulf countries as well as the principal consumers of Iraqi oil in Asia and Europe could surely raise funds for this purpose. The prospect of sharing in this revenue, which Saddam Hussein presently controls, also offers a powerful reason for Iraq's different ethnic groups to retain their allegiance to the state.

The United States may need to occupy Iraq for some time. Though U.N., European and Arab forces will, as in Afghanistan, contribute troops, the principal responsibility will doubtless fall to the country that liberates Baghdad. According to one estimate, initially as many as 75,000 U.S. troops may be required to police the war's aftermath, at a cost of $16 billion a year. As other countries' forces arrive, and as Iraq rebuilds its economy and political system, that force could probably be drawn down to several thousand soldiers after a year or two.

After Saddam Hussein has been defeated and Iraq occupied, installing a decent and democratic government in Baghdad should be a manageable task for the United States. But not according to some realists. *Time* columnist Michael Elliott scoffs, "The President looked forward to a day when 'the people of Iraq' can join a 'democratic Afghanistan and a democratic Palestine,' inspiring reforms throughout the Muslim world.... Yet there is a problem with Bush's vision: it will have to be imposed from the outside." In a similar vein, the Brooking Institution's Middle East analyst, Shibley Telhami, writes in the *New York Times* that "Democracy cannot be imposed through military forces, even if force is used successfully to oust antidemocratic dictators."

Really? What about Japan, Germany, Austria, Italy, Grenada, the Dominican Republic and Panama? These are only a few of the nations whose democratic systems were at first "imposed" by American arms. Furthermore, Iraq, more perhaps than any other nation in the region, is ripe for democracy. For evidence, one need look no further than northern Iraq, where, under an umbrella of American air patrols, the Iraqi opposition already presides over a thriving democracy. Iraq possesses some of the highest literacy rates in the region, an urbanized middle class, and other demographic measures that typically conduce to democracy. Indeed, the exile umbrella group, the Iraqi National Congress, is already working on the shape of Baghdad's postwar government. According to INC founding member Laith Kubba, its principal aims will be to "create a constitution assembly with a coherent agenda, hold a free and fair referendum on ratification, and, ultimately seek power through the ballot box." The Bush administration, too, has been drawing up plans for a democratic Iraq—a nation represented, in the words of Vice President Cheney, by "a government that is democratic and pluralistic . . . where the human rights of every ethnic and religious group are recognized and protected."

The establishment of such a state should have powerful reverberations in the Arab world, where not one country qualifies as a democracy. *New York Times* columnist Thomas Friedman, for example, supports invading Iraq because "what the Arab world desperately needs is a model that works—a progressive Arab regime that by its sheer existence would create pressure and inspiration for gradual democratization and modernization around the region." The vista that "the first Arab democracy," as Paul Wolfowitz puts it, could open up would be stunning. It could "prove to be as large as anything that has happened in the Middle East since the fall of the Ottoman Empire," says Iraq scholar Kanan Makiya.

Iraq's experience of liberal democratic rule in turn could increase the pressure already being felt by Teheran's mullahs to open that society. Iraq's model will be eyed warily by Saudi Arabia's theocrats to the south, where male unemployment stands at 30 percent, population growth is rapid, and the populace is restive for change. Meanwhile, Iraq could even replace Saudi Arabia as the key American ally and source of oil in the region. A democratic Iraq would also encourage the region's already liberalizing regimes—such as those in Qatar, Morocco and Jordan—to continue on their paths toward democracy.

Then, too, a Baghdad under American supervision would surely improve its relations with the region's other democracies, Turkey and Israel. Arguing exactly this point, Vice President Cheney predicts that when Saddam falls, "the freedom-loving peoples of the region will have a chance to promote the values that can bring lasting peace."

When speaking of democracy in the broader Muslim world, however, one encounters yet another, more serious objection from critics of the Bush Doctrine—namely, that Islam and democracy are inherently incompatible. Adam Garfinkle, editor of the *National Interest,* writes that anything America does is "unlikely to change the contemporary Arab view of liberal democracy as an alien Western idea at a time when Arab societies are struggling to cope with Western-wrought modernity." And, just as Colin Powell dismissed the idea of a "desert democracy where people read *The Federalist Papers* along with the Koran," Middle East expert Graham Fuller scoffs at the notion that modern liberal governance could take root in the Islamic world "from imported Western modules of 'instant democracy.'"

As it happens, this line of reasoning mirrors exactly the logic that U.S. scholars and policymakers applied to every other formerly undemocratic region of the world. "I doubt that democracy U.S.-style can be exported," the Latin Americanist Howard Wiarda argued in the 1980s. "I doubt that Latin America wants it, or wants it all that much." Thirty years earlier, Joseph Grew, the State Department's chief Japan expert, had cautioned President Truman that "the best we can hope for is a constitutional monarchy, experience having shown that democracy in Japan would never work." At various points since World War II, American policymakers have made the same point about Germany, Russia, East Asia and South America. And now that the tide of democracy has swept over each of these regions, they are again making the same point about the one region that it has yet to touch.

But is the Islamic world immune from the appeal of democratization? There is an important distinction to be made between the Arab world, which is overwhelmingly Muslim, and the Muslim world, not all of which is Arab. In the latter, from Turkey to Indonesia, democracy has indeed made dramatic advances over the past decades. Members of the Bush team—including Paul Wolfowitz and Undersecretary of State Paula Dobriansky—have made the point forcefully. According to

Dobriansky, those who argue that democracy "is not realistic in the Muslim world have been listening to Muslim politicians, civil society leaders, academics, and religious authorities who are increasingly arguing that it is not only possible, indeed it is essential." Or as President Bush himself put it, "The peoples of the Islamic nations want and deserve the same freedoms and opportunities as people in every nation, and their governments should listen to their hopes." The problem, in fact, is less the Islamic world than the Arab world.

There is today not a single Arab state that qualifies as a democracy. The "Arab Human Development Report 2002," compiled under the auspices of the United Nations and sponsored by the Arab Fund for Economic and Social Development, examines why this is the case. "The wave of democracy that transformed governance in most of Latin America and East Asia in the 1980s, and Eastern Europe and much of Central Asia in the late 1980s and early 1990s, has barely reached the Arab States. This freedom deficit undermines human development and is one of the most painful manifestations of lagging political development." Among the explanations the report offers for this pitiful state of affairs is a traditional Arab culture at odds with modernization, overwhelming illiteracy rates, poverty, stagnant economic growth, weak civil society and, most important, the persistence in every Arab state of "a powerful executive branch that exerts significant control over all other branches of the state, being in some cases free from institutional checks and balances."

Despite this Arab self-indictment, Senator Chuck Hagel complains, "I detect a dangerous arrogance and a sort of 'Pax Americana' vision which holds that we are more powerful, richer, and smarter than the rest of the world, and we are going to go forth and impose democracy." But promoting democracy in the Middle East is not a matter of national egoism. It has become a matter of national well-being, even survival. On September 11, the Arab world's predicament became our own. Not only has Arab repression fueled Islamist terror movements and anti-American extremism; the very regimes we have been propping up have directly encouraged these forces as a way to deflect popular anger from their palace gates. The eminent historian John Lewis Gaddis writes:

The intersection of radicalism with technology the world witnessed on that terrible morning means that the persistence of authoritarianism anywhere can breed resentments that can provoke terrorism that can do us grievous harm. There is a compellingly realistic reason now to complete the idealistic task Woodrow Wilson began more than eight decades ago: the world must be made safe for democracy, because otherwise democracy will not be safe in the world.

Having created a domestic audience for Islamic extremism through their repressive policies, the regimes most directly threatened by Islamist movements have co-opted and sanctioned their worst elements. This is particularly true of Saudi Arabia, parts of whose royal family have funded Osama bin Laden and other anti-American terror groups, on the one hand, while benefiting from the protection of the United States, on the other.

When it came to the Middle East, Washington upheld a special bargain: Arab dictators provided the United States with oil, basing rights and counterweight to Soviet and other hostile influences; in return, the United States overlooked the depredations they inflicted on their citizens and their involvement with Islamist groups. For all his efforts elsewhere, President Reagan never promoted democracy in the Middle East. Neither did the first Bush administration—even in Kuwait, a country that American soldiers died to liberate. For its part, Bill Clinton's team proceeded on the assumption that, as his Middle East point man Martin Indyk recalled, "moderate Arab states would provide the U.S. military with access to bases and facilities ... ; in return, Washington would not exert significant pressure for domestic change." The present administration, until quite recently, honored the agreement as well—for example, by refusing to press the Saudis to cooperate in the September 11 investigation or even to allow us to launch raids against bin Laden from Saudi territory. Invoking a version of Jeane Kirkpatrick's "Dictatorships and Double Standards" argument, members of the Bush team argued that, yes, "friendly" Arab dictatorships were unpalatable, but their potential successors would be even worse. Nor have those "friendly" dictators been shy about reminding the Bush team of their likely replacements. Thus, in a letter to President Bush last year, Saudi Arabia's Crown Prince

Abdullah pointed out that if the United States failed to be more sensitive to his regime's plight, the royal family could "suffer the fate of the Shah of Iran."

As applied to the likes of Saudi Arabia and Egypt, however, Franklin Roosevelt's description of Nicaragua's Anastasio Somoza—"He may be a son of a bitch. But he's our son of a bitch"—fails to persuade. To begin with, countries like Saudi Arabia are not, in fact, *ours* at all. Far from being our clients, as Somoza once was, they not only have helped to create the problem of Islamist radicalism, but actively abet it. During the Cold War, when the risks were at least as great as they are now, the Reagan administration devised a way to further democracy from El Salvador to the Philippines without bringing its foes to power. Then, as now, skeptics cautioned that the devil we knew was safer than the alternative. They were wrong then. They are wrong now.

In terms of concrete policy initiatives, the efforts to build democracy in the Middle East have so far been modest—a boost in funds for the U.S. Agency for International Development to promote democracy; grants for the National Endowment for Democracy to do the same; a State Department–run program to fund democratization efforts in Morocco, Bahrain and Qatar; and the creation of a radio network to bring accurate and fair news coverage to a region not known for either. But in terms of rhetoric, which usually precedes policy, the administration has gone much further. Further, indeed, than any of its predecessors. "We reject the condescending view that freedom will not grow in the soil of the Middle East—or that Muslims somehow do not share in the desire to be free," Condoleezza Rice said last October. Backing up these words with deeds, the Bush team has offered support for pro-democracy demonstrators in Iran, insisted on political reforms in the Palestinian Authority, and censured President Hosni Mubarak for his treatment of democracy activists in Egypt.

Pledging that the United States "will use this moment of opportunity to extend the benefits of freedom across the globe," Bush is equally strong in his support for democracy beyond the Middle East:

> The United States possesses unprecedented—and unequaled—strength and influence in the world. Sustained by faith in the principles of liberty, and the value of a free society, this position comes

> with unparalleled responsibilities, obligations and opportunities.
> The great strength of this nation must be used to promote a bal-
> ance of power that favors freedom.

This proposition seems inarguable. But according to critics on both
the right and the left, our "preoccupation" with democratizing other
states is flawed by the parochial assumption that our principles are
universal ones; such narrow chauvinism inevitably leads to dangerous "crusades" to make the world over, and derives from a uniquely
lethal American mixture of naïveté and hubris. In one sense, such a
critique contains a kernel of truth. Exporting democracy *does* further
America's vital interests. But it does this by fulfilling our most cher-
ished ideals—chief among them a belief that people should not be
governed without their consent. As the Bush national security strategy puts it, "No people on earth yearn to be oppressed, aspire to servi-
tude, or eagerly await the midnight knock of the secret police."

The universality of American principles has its strategic uses as
well. By defining our aims in democratic, rather than in specifically
American, terms, U.S. policies may attract wider support. Characterizing the U.S. effort to oust Saddam as "a war for oil," critics of the
Bush Doctrine at home and abroad try to portray the United States as
a bully state intoxicated by the arrogance of power. To the degree that
we phrase—and wage—this war as a war for democracy, the effect
among Middle Easterners will be far different. A "balance of power
that favors freedom" also lends coherence to what often seems like an
incoherent American approach to the world. Undertakings from the
wars in Kosovo and Iraq to U.S. assistance to Israel and Taiwan—which
at first glance bear little relation to one another—take on the qualities of a coherent worldview under this umbrella. "Cast in these terms,"
writes Stanford University scholar Michael McFaul, "Muslims and
Christians, Americans and Iranians, Arabs and Italians can all be on
the same side. Framed in these terms, the enemy is also much larger
than Islamic totalitarians and includes all those who oppose liberty,
be they dictators in North Korea or sheiks in Saudi Arabia."

The strategic value of democracy is reflected in a truth of international politics: Democracies rarely, if ever, wage war against one
another. Why? One reason was identified by Immanuel Kant:

> [When] the consent of the citizens is required to decide whether or not war should be declared, it is very natural that they will have a great hesitation in embarking on so dangerous an enterprise.... But under a constitution ... which is ... not republican, it is the simplest thing in the world to go to war. For the head of state is not a fellow citizen, but the owner of the state, and war will not force him to make the slightest sacrifice.

The ethics and institutions of democracy encourage compromise and other norms that democratic states then apply to their relations with one another. Nondemocratic states, needless to say, do not. Or, as Woodrow Wilson put it in 1917, "A steadfast concert of peace can never be maintained except by a partnership of democratic nations. No autocratic government could be trusted to keep faith within it or observe its covenants."

A century of fighting fascist dictators in Germany, Italy and Japan, communist dictators in Korea and Vietnam, neofascist dictators in the Balkans and Iraq, and for that matter a narco-trafficking dictator in Central America has alerted all but the most obdurate policymakers to the fact that the character of regimes—not diplomatic agreements or multilateral institutions—are the key to peace and stability. The strategy of focusing on regime change to foster democracy, writes political scientist G. John Ikenberry, "is a strategy based on the very realistic view that the political character of other states has an enormous impact on the ability of the United States to ensure its security and economic interests." For the United States, then, a straightforward argument from self-interest follows naturally: The more democratic the world becomes, the more likely it is to be congenial to America.

Tactics for pursuing democratization may vary according to circumstance. In some cases, the policy might focus on rebel groups, along the lines of the Reagan Doctrine as it was applied in Nicaragua and elsewhere in the 1980s. In other cases, it might mean support for dissidents by either overt or covert means, which yielded such positive results in countries such as Poland and South Korea. The tactics may or may not succeed immediately, but their purpose ought to be clear. When it comes to dealing with tyrannical regimes, especially those with the power to do us or our allies harm, the United States should seek transformation, not coexistence.

The idea that the United States can "do business" with any regime, no matter how odious and hostile to American principles, is both morally and strategically dubious. Relationships with tyrannical regimes are inherently difficult to sustain. The force of American ideals and American power tends inevitably to corrode the pillars on which authoritarian and totalitarian regimes rest. To buttress their legitimacy, such regimes therefore resort frequently to provocation, either with arms buildups designed to intimidate both the United States and its allies, as in the case of China and North Korea, or by plots for regional conquest, as in the case of Iraq and Serbia. Unable to acquire legitimacy through the consent of their own oppressed citizens, such states seek the more superficial authority that comes from demonizing an external enemy. The Chinese government, for instance, knows there can be no real "strategic partnership" with the United States. The Iranian government knows there can be no true "normalization" with the democratic world. Saddam Hussein knows he cannot simply give up the weapons of mass destruction he has compiled. The price of such accommodations would be the collapse of their regimes.

Promoting democracy is a pragmatic goal in that it makes the world more congenial to America. But while it is a sound strategy, it is also America's particular inheritance. Its tenets are enshrined in the country's Declaration of Independence. Its substance is defined by the Constitution. And its influence has shaped two centuries of U.S. foreign policy. Not only is the United States a beacon of liberal democracy; every one of this country's leaders—whether arguing that America's international behavior should exemplify these democratic ideals or that the United States could best inspire others through the practice of these ideals at home—has recognized the special role that America's principles play in its conduct abroad.

This uniquely American interest in democracy is precisely what troubles so many of Bush's critics on the left. Doubtful that the United States is capable of installing a "democratic government in a place that has never known one," former Gore national security advisor Leon Fuerth warns that the attempt to do so may lead to "a dangerous intoxication with American power." The democracy promoters in the Bush administration belong to "that most dangerous breed of men, utopians," says *New York Times* columnist Anthony Lewis. In a similar vein, Harvard professor Stanley Hoffman, who only a few years ago was writing in defense of "morality in foreign policy," cannot understand why the United States would want to change "countries that have no past experience of democracy and where repressive regimes face no experienced or cohesive opposition."

At the beginning of the twentieth century, Woodrow Wilson launched a crusade to "make the world safe for democracy." His successors from FDR to JFK never questioned that goal. But in the long aftermath of Vietnam, this vision became tarnished. Liberals in particular questioned whether the United States had any right to judge its own system superior to others or, for that matter, to assert American influence. They did not deny the benefits of democracy, but they did question the principal means used to accomplish it—namely, American power. Thus, when the Carter team spoke out on behalf of democracy, it did so most vocally in the case of allies, such as Iran and Nicaragua, who were confronting insurgencies at home, rather than criticize the Soviet Union and its satellites. A deep-seated reluctance to judge others and a lingering skepticism about America's founding ideals also led liberals to emphasize the promotion of universal "social" and "economic" rights over democracy—the latter being too closely identified with the United States. "The Cold War led us astray," explained Clinton's public diplomacy czar, Joseph Duffey. "We got into a crusading mentality," whereby it "somehow made us feel better to throw messages at other countries."

Echoing George McGovern, who claimed during his 1972 campaign that "forces beyond our control will have the most to do with shaping the political arrangements of the future," and Jimmy Carter, whose national security advisor, Zbigniew Brzezinski, looked forward to "an age in which technology and electronics ... are increasingly becoming the principal determinants of ... the global outlook of society," the Clinton team decided that vast, impersonal forces could achieve many of the traditional aims of American policy. Specifically, democracy would be furthered not by America's political activism, but rather by the forces of "interdependence," by which the Clinton administration meant international trade. According to the Clinton team, focusing on international commerce not only made good economic sense, but could help accomplish the traditional aims of U.S. foreign policy, chief among them democratization. Or as national security advisor Sandy Berger put it in 1997, "the fellow travelers of the new global economy—computers and modems, faxes and photocopiers, increased contacts and binding contracts—carry with them the seeds of change." After officially "delinking" human rights and trade considerations in China in 1994, Clinton offered assurances that commerce and technology would suffice as "a force for change in China, exposing China to our ideas and our ideals."

The hope of leaving the task of democratization to the market, however, ensnarled the Clinton team in moral complications to which it could provide no adequate response. The Clinton White House characterized its approach to foreign affairs as "pragmatic neo-Wilsonianism," but Woodrow Wilson entered office with the explicit intention of putting an end to the "dollar diplomacy" of the Taft administration. Moreover, the logic of the Clinton team's approach to democratization was quickly revealed to have things exactly backward. Comforted that it could promote democracy by means of sheer acquisitiveness, the administration disregarded human rights violations in countries where American corporations happened to do business. And far from tempering those violations, the expansion of trade ties with countries like China and Pakistan coincided with a worsening of their human rights records. This subordination of political principle to the expansion of economic ties also led to the justified charge of American hypocrisy. As the French newspaper *Le Monde* noted in an editorial, "The Chinese case destroys the American pretension to universality on human rights." Far from spreading democracy, under the terms of "interdependence," the international conduct of the United States was becoming indistinguishable from that of the Europeans.

The Bush Doctrine rejects the complacent assumption that "engagement" will suffice to promote democratization. It also acknowledges that democracy is a political choice, an act of will. Someone, not something, must create it. Often that someone is a single leader— a Lech Walensa, a King Juan Carlos, a Václav Havel. Other times, the pressure for democracy comes for a political opposition movement—the African National Congress in South Africa, Solidarity in Poland, or the marchers in Tiananmen Square. But history suggests that it comes most effectively from the United States.

During the 1980s, America applied diplomatic and economic pressure to repressive regimes from Poland to South Africa; intervened to prevent military coups in the Philippines, Peru, El Salvador, Honduras and Bolivia; and bluntly enshrined human rights and democracy in official policy. The United States played a pivotal and direct role in democratizing countries like South Korea and Taiwan. Appropriately enough, the decade closed with democracy activists erecting a facsimile of the Statue of Liberty in Tiananmen Square. Christopher Patten, the last British governor of nearby Hong Kong, observed: "American power and leadership have been more responsible than most other factors in rescuing freedom in the second half of this century."

To argue that the United States, having come so far, should now leave that task to technology or commerce or even international organizations is absurd. To argue that America should do so because it has no "right" to impose its will on others is wrong. "The Communist leaders say, 'Don't interfere in our internal affairs. Let us strangle our citizens in peace and quiet,'" Alexandr Solzhenitsyn once wrote. "But I tell you: Interfere more and more. Interfere as much as you can. We beg you to come and interfere."

Solzhenitsyn's admonition is of course as unwelcome to conservative realists as it is to leftist skeptics of American power. While many of these realists played a key role during the Cold War and supported the main thrust of U.S. policy during this era—warning Americans away from the delusions of both liberal accommodation and isolationism, supporting a robust level of defense expenditure, and alerting policymakers to the threat that Soviet expansionism posed—they were never sympathetic to the idealism that infused that policy. Early on in the Cold War, theologian Reinhold Niebuhr complained that "we are still inclined to pretend that our power is exercised by a peculiarly virtuous nation," while his fellow realist George Kennan went so far as to compare American democracy to "one of those pre-historic monsters with a body as long as a room and a brain the size of a pin." What the realists feared was not so much the mechanics of American democracy at home—although they often had reservations about that, too—but rather what they perceived to be a messianic impulse that could lead America to upset the balance of power between it and the Soviet Union. Awash in this relativism, Hans Morgenthau characterized American democracy and Soviet communism as merely two variations of the same "nationalistic universalism," which sought "for one nation and one state the right to impose its own valuations and standards of action upon all other nations." What Americans ought to recognize, Kennan recommended, was that "no people can be the judge of another's domestic institutions and requirements."

Blinded by this line of reasoning, the realists never anticipated that "the domestic institutions and requirements" of both the Soviet Union and the United States would be precisely what brought an end to the Cold War. Just as the internal contradictions of communism contributed to the demise of the Soviet Union and its satellites, so did the allure and success of American democracy offer a better alternative to the inhabitants of communist nations. The principles of liberal democracy had also supported the sacrifices that Americans were willing to make during four decades of cold war. Idealism, argued Robert Osgood in a rebuttal of Morgenthau, was an "indispensable spur to reason." It turned out that communism could not compete with liberal democracy materially, politically or ethically. Communism as an idea could not even outlast the coercive power that made it into a global ideology. Liberal democracy, by contrast, has been profoundly vindicated and its appeal continues to grow.

This dramatic vindication notwithstanding, many realists still regard the idea of America using its power to promote change of regime in nations ruled by dictators as dangerous utopianism. Rather than prompt second thoughts, today's realists have somehow managed to locate in one of history's most lopsided victories the seeds of an even greater defeat. Hence, where a few years earlier Harvard University's Samuel Huntington conceded that Americans "have a special interest in the development of a global environment congenial to democracy," by the mid-1990s he was condemning U.S. efforts to promote such an environment as "false," "immoral" and "danger-ous." In an identical vein, the Nixon Center's Dmitri Simes and for-mer NATO ambassador Robert Ellsworth claim, "The assumption that our values are universal is false because it is demonstrably untrue; immoral because of what would be necessary to make non-Western people adopt Western institutions and culture; and dangerous because it could lead to war."

At first glance, the complaints of today's realists bear even less scrutiny than those of their predecessors. After all, during the Cold War democracy's global appeal had yet to be empirically proven, and if idealism acted as a spur to reasonable action, so, for the realists, did the threat of nuclear annihilation. Today, with the disappearance of the Soviet Union and the rapid advance of democracy, their admo-nitions seem more puzzling. There is something perverse in contin-uing to doubt the efficacy of promoting democratic change abroad in light of the record of the past three decades. After we have already seen dictatorships toppled by democratic forces in such seemingly unlikely places as the Philippines, Indonesia, Chile, Nicaragua, Paraguay, Taiwan and South Korea, how utopian is it to imagine a change of regime in a place like Iraq? For that matter, how utopian is it to work for the fall of the Communist Party in China after a far more powerful and stable oligarchy fell in the Soviet Union? With democratic change sweeping the world at an unprecedented rate over the past decades, is it truly "realistic" to insist that we quit now?

NINE

From Ambivalence to Leadership

The final and most controversial pillar of the Bush Doctrine is its commitment to American preeminence. The insistence that the United States must prevent potential adversaries from "surpassing, or equaling, the power of the United States" has elicited an outcry along the Eastern seaboard. "The vision laid out in the Bush document is a vision of what used to be called, when we believed it to be the Soviet ambition, world domination," Hendrik Hertzberg claims in the *New Yorker,* managing in one sentence to indict the U.S. and exonerate the USSR. What the national security strategy is fundamentally about, echoes Al Gore, is "glorifying the notion of dominance." Well, what is wrong with dominance, in the service of sound principles and high ideals?

"The Bush administration has clearly broken with the internationalist premises that have been accepted by every other administration since World War II, with the exception of Reagan's first," complains Frances Fitzgerald in the *New York Review of Books.* But this is simply wrong. Far from breaking with the premises of postwar national security policy, the Bush Doctrine harkens back to the tenets that guided American policy through the most successful phases of that period. The era commenced in 1947 with a congressional address by Harry Truman in which he allowed the "frank recognition that totalitarian regimes imposed on free people, by direct or indirect aggression, undermine the foundations of international peace and hence the security of the United States." In defining this new era, Bush, like Truman before him, has resorted to the language of American exceptionalism, insisting that the "requirements of freedom apply fully" to all and that the United States will promote these requirements tirelessly. Just as on

March 12, 1947, Truman unveiled the doctrine that carries his name, pledging to confront Soviet expansionism wherever it emerged and to promote freedom, so on June 1, 2002, Bush previewed the doctrine that carries his name, pledging to preempt threats wherever they arose and to promote freedom. One president relied on containment and the other on preemption, but the Truman and Bush Doctrines share a common purpose: Both offer roadmaps for American leadership, backed up by American power and culminating in the spread of American ideals. In fact, both doctrines trace their lineage back to principles that animated American foreign policy even before the Cold War.

"[T]his is a period not just of grave danger, but of enormous opportunity," says Condoleezza Rice, " . . . a period akin to 1945 to 1947, when American leadership expanded the number of free and democratic states—Japan and Germany among the great powers—to create a new balance of power that favored freedom." Just as sensible Americans after World War II did not imagine that the United States should retreat from global involvement and await the rise of the next Nazi Germany, so the Bush team has recognized that in the aftermath of September 11 its charge is to shape the international environment to prevent the next threat from arising in the first place. We often forget that the plans for a postwar order devised by American foreign policy makers in the early 1940s were not simply aimed at containing the Soviet Union, which many of them still viewed as a potential partner. Rather, those policymakers were looking backward to the circumstances that had led to the catastrophe of global conflict. Their purpose was to construct a more stable international order than the one that had imploded in 1939; an economic system that furthered the aim of international stability by promoting growth and free trade; and a framework for international security that, although it placed too much faith in the willingness of the Soviet Union to work with the United States, rested ultimately on the fact that American power had become the keystone in the arch of world order.

Men like James Forrestal and Dean Acheson believed the United States had supplanted Great Britain as the world's leader and that, as Forrestal put it in 1941, "America must be the dominant power of the twentieth century." Henry Luce spoke for most influential Americans inside and outside the Roosevelt administration when he insisted that it had fallen to the United States not only to win the war against Germany and Japan, but to create an "international moral order" that would spread American principles—and in the process avoid the catastrophe of a third world war. Such thinking was reflected in Roosevelt's Atlantic Charter and, more concretely, in the creation of the United Nations in 1945.

Thus, well before the Soviet Union had emerged as the great challenge to American security and American principles, American leaders had arrived at the conclusion that it would be necessary for the United States to deter aggression globally, whoever the aggressor might be, in order to build a safer world. In fact, during the war years they were at least as worried about the possible reemergence of Germany and Japan as about the Soviets. John Lewis Gaddis has summarized American thinking in the years between 1941 and 1946 in this way:

> The American president and his key advisers were determined to secure the United States against whatever dangers might confront it after victory, but they lacked a clear sense of what those might be or where they might arise. Their thinking about post-war security was, as a consequence, more general than specific.

Few influential government officials, moreover, were under the illusion that "collective security" and the United Nations could be counted on to keep the peace. In 1945 Harry Truman declared that the United States had become "one of the most powerful forces for good on earth," and the task now was to "keep it so" and to "lead the world to peace and prosperity." The United States had "achieved a world leadership which does not depend solely upon our military and naval might," Truman declared. But it was his intention, despite demobilization, to ensure that the United States would remain "the greatest naval power on earth" and would maintain "one of the most powerful air forces in the world." Americans, Truman said, would use "our military strength solely to preserve the peace of the world. For we now know that this is the only sure way to make our own freedom secure."

The unwillingness to sustain the level of military spending and preparedness required to fulfill this expansive vision was a failure of

American foreign policy in the immediate aftermath of the war. But Stalin's drawing of the Iron Curtain and the outbreak of the war in Korea reawakened Americans to the need for an assertive and forward-leaning foreign policy. But while the United States promptly rose to meet these challenges, a certain intellectual clarity was lost in the transition from the immediate postwar years to the beginning of the Cold War. The original goal of promoting and defending a decent world order became conflated with the goal of meeting the challenge of Soviet power. The United States adopted policies it would have pursued even in the absence of a Soviet challenge—playing a large role in Europe, Asia and the Middle East; upholding basic norms of international behavior; promoting democratic reform where possible and advancing American principles abroad. All of these ideals became associated with the strategy of containing the Soviet Union, and therefore with the strategy that led America into Southeast Asia.

If anything, the Bush Doctrine signals a return to this earlier era, when Munich, not Vietnam, was the cautionary lesson and admonitions about the "arrogance of power" and the perils of "judging others" had little traction among U.S. policymakers. In a 1951 address explaining America's participation in the Korean War, President Truman insisted that if the allies "had followed the right policies in the 1930s—if the free countries had acted together to crush the aggression of the dictators, and if they had acted at the beginning when the aggression was small—there probably would have been no World War II. If history has taught us anything, it is that aggression anywhere in the world is a threat to peace everywhere in the world." Today, too, American policymakers are drawing the same lesson: resist aggression with force if necessary, and sooner rather than later. "Hitler had indicated what he intended to do," Defense Secretary Donald Rumsfeld told an interviewer in 2001, adding that he should have "been stopped early, as he might have been . . . at minimal cost."

If the Bush Doctrine really does "break" from the premises of recent national security policy, then, it is only because it departs decisively from the legacy of Vietnam. A recent *Newsweek* profile of Donald Rumsfeld revealed something striking about him, and to a degree about the Bush Doctrine: "Rumsfeld is a product of a time and generation that was long in eclipse but whose outlook and attitudes are now making a comeback at the highest levels of the U.S. government." The article continues, "The decision on whether to invade Iraq, seen through the prism of Rumsfeld's background and experience, can be seen as a clash between the values of the Greatest Generation and the early cold warriors and the baby boomers who came to power after Watergate and Vietnam." The profile concludes with a quote from Henry Kissinger, who observed that "[Rumsfeld] is trying to bring back the duty of service and American responsibility, to beat back the attitudes of the Vietnam generation that was focused on American imperfection and limitations."

Those attitudes survived the demise of the Soviet Union. On the left, where writer Noemie Emery has observed "it is always 1968, the dark night of the American soul," the Vietnam syndrome returned during Operation Desert Storm. It persisted through the Clinton administration, as veterans of the McGovern campaign wrung their hands about repeating Vietnam's mistakes in Bosnia and Kosovo— so much so that Balkans troubleshooter Richard Holbrooke felt compelled to point out that "Bosnia was not Vietnam, the Serbs were not the Vietcong, and Belgrade was not Hanoi." The ghost of Vietnam walks again today. "I kept thinking of one thing: Vietnam," writes Anthony Lewis in the *New York Review of Books,* echoing his objections to the Gulf War a decade earlier. "Iraq is a large, modern, heavily urbanized country. If we bomb it apart, are we going to be wise enough to put it back together?"

On the right, the Nixonian strategy of avoiding another Vietnam by focusing on narrowly conceived vital interests also continued well into the 1990s. Though he invoked the Munich analogy and even likened Saddam Hussein to Hitler, President George H. W. Bush pledged that he had "learned from Vietnam" and conducted the Gulf War accordingly—halting it once the "vital interest" of Kuwaiti oil had been secured, and leaving thousands of Iraqis to be slaughtered by the "Hitler" whom the United States had decided to leave in power. After having boasted that "we've kicked the Vietnam syndrome once and for all," not a year later Bush opposed intervening in Bosnia's "guerrilla warfare" because "We've lived through that once already." Even George W. Bush, at the 2000 Republican National Convention, admonished his audience to "remember the lessons of Vietnam."

Politicians are not the only ones who still suffer from the Vietnam syndrome. The American military establishment over which Rumsfeld presides has yet to recover from the war. "Vietnam," explains strategist Eliot Cohen, "has become the defense establishment's morality play, a cautionary tale of civilian meddling, military timidity, and ensuing—but unnecessary—disaster." The bureaucratic lessons of this morality play were first articulated by Caspar Weinberger, Reagan's defense secretary, who spelled out a restrictive set of criteria for the use of force. Colin Powell later enshrined those criteria in the doctrine that now carries his name. The Powell Doctrine addresses more than just how to fight wars; it also addresses *when* to fight them—namely, for "vital interests," not for "half-baked reasons" like "nation-building" and "humanitarianism," which call up the specter of Vietnam. Powell summarizes his doctrine this way: "Is the national interest at stake? If the answer is yes, go in, and go in to win. Otherwise, stay out."

This may sound reasonable enough. Invoking the Powell Doctrine and the war that inspired it, however, America's senior generals have opposed nearly every intervention that the United States has undertaken in the post–Cold War era—Iraq, Bosnia, Kosovo and now Iraq again. "In none of these recent foreign crises," Powell wrote of the Clinton-era conflicts in his autobiography, "have we had a vital interest such as we had after Iraq's invasion of Kuwait and the resulting threat to Saudi Arabia and the free flow of oil." Never mind that Powell opposed the Gulf War, too. In rhetoric, the Powell Doctrine sounds powerful. In practice, it is a template for inaction.

When it is governed by the Vietnam analogy, the United States almost always suffers setbacks. There is a simple reason for this: Our policymakers may be consumed by the lessons of Vietnam, but the rest of the world plays by Munich rules. Hence, while Nixon and Kissinger consigned the Third World to the back burner in the aftermath of Vietnam, Moscow redoubled its efforts to expand Soviet influence in Africa, the Middle East and East Asia. And while President Carter derived from Vietnam the lesson that the United States should not "interfere in the internal affairs of another nation," the Soviet Union was busy invading Afghanistan and establishing a proxy in Central America. Assuming, too, that the United States had lost its nerve, both Saddam Hussein and Slobodan Milosevic invoked the legacy of Vietnam to explain why America would not halt their aggressions.

In fact, as a guide for how and when to use force in the post–Cold War era, the Vietnam analogy has proved next to useless. In many instances, much as the left resists acknowledging it, all that stands between civility and genocide, order and mayhem, is American power. Strict adherence to the lessons of Vietnam means no peacekeeping missions, no punitive air strikes, no humanitarian interventions—in short, no operation that proceeds from any principle other than the narrowest self-interest. As for the conservative lessons of Vietnam, the brand of foreign policy restraint that they encourage is even more out of place in today's world. The definition of vital interests as consisting merely of oil wells, sea lanes and canals would, if enshrined in official policy, translate into the abdication of American leadership. When America refused to act in Bosnia, for instance, the humanitarian crisis quickly began to threaten the stability of the Atlantic alliance, one of the most vital of American interests. Realists may not like it, but the United States remains the hinge of the international system. And when it sits idly by in the face of threats to that system, international order erodes. Quickly. In recent history, it has been excessive American reticence, not bellicosity, which has led to more problems and greater dangers.

Like the cold warriors of the pre-Vietnam era, members of the Bush team recognize that the present era offers both crisis and opportunity. In their view, the United States must pursue two goals at once: first, the promotion of a world order conducive to American interests and principles; and second, a defense against the most immediate and menacing obstacle to achieving that order. In other words, fighting an unconventional war on terrorism does not absolve U.S. foreign policy of its traditional aims. But the discovery last year that America must still contend with cruel and resourceful foes has generated a certain fatalism about broad foreign policy goals, particularly among elites. "We no longer have the luxury of thinking about U.S. national security primarily in terms of protecting American allies and interests abroad," says Michele Flournoy, a senior advisor at the Center for Strategic and International Studies. "We need to give far more serious attention to protecting the U.S. homeland." That we do. But this hardly relieves the United States of its obligation to defend Taiwan from China, to stand by Israel and our European and Asian allies, and to defend American principles abroad. A failure to mind the broader ends of U.S. foreign policy could leave us even more vulnerable than before to the conventional threats that consumed our attention until September 11.

The events following 9-11 have not altered the fundamental purposes of American foreign policy. On the contrary, the administration's war against terror falls squarely within the tradition of America's grand strategy. Nor, in its essentials, does that strategy respond to anything more than a simple recognition of fact. The conceit of the Bush administration's critics is that America's position in the world amounts to something other than global preeminence. The United States has assumed an unprecedented position of power and influence in the world. By the traditional measures of national power, the United States holds a position unmatched since Rome dominated the Mediterranean world. American military power dwarfs that of any other nation, both in its war-fighting capabilities and in its ability to intervene in conflicts anywhere in the world on short notice. Meanwhile, the American economic precepts of liberal capitalism and free trade have become almost universally accepted as the best model for creating wealth, and the United States itself stands at the center of the international economic order. The American political precepts of liberal democracy have spread across continents and cultures as other peoples cast off or modify autocratic methods of governance and opt for, or at least pay lip service to, the American principles of individual rights and freedoms.

Moreover, unlike past imperial powers, if the United States has created a Pax Americana, it is not built on colonial conquest or economic aggrandizement. "America has no empire to extend or utopia to establish," President Bush said in his West Point speech. Rather, what upholds today's world order is America's benevolent influence — nurtured, to be sure, by American power, but also by emulation and the recognition around the world that American ideals are genuinely universal. As a consequence, when the world's sole superpower commits itself to norms of international conduct — for democracy, for human rights, against aggression, against weapons proliferation — it means that successful challenges to American power will invariably weaken those American-created norms. Were we—through humility, self-abnegation or a narrow conception of the national interest—to retreat from the position that history has bequeathed us, the turmoil that would soon follow would surely reach our shores.

Even if the threat posed by Iraq were to disappear tomorrow, that would not relieve us of the need to play a strong and active role in the world. Nor would it absolve us of the responsibilities that fate has placed on our shoulders. Given the dangers that currently exist, and given the certainty that unknown perils await us over the horizon, there can be no respite from this burden. The maintenance of a decent and hospitable international order requires continued American leadership in resisting, and where possible undermining, aggressive dictators and hostile ideologies; in supporting American interests and liberal democratic principles; and in providing assistance to those struggling against the more extreme manifestations of human evil. If America refrains from shaping this order, we can be sure that others will shape it in ways that reflect neither our interests nor our values.

Absent the United States, who else could uphold decency in the world? Europe? Having engaged in fratricidal conflict twice in the twentieth century, and then taken shelter under an American umbrella during the Cold War, much of Europe has responded to the challenges of the post–Cold War era with a mixture of pettiness, impotence and moral lassitude. Having proclaimed the 1990s the "hour of Europe," its leaders spent the decade failing to deal with ethnic cleansing on their own continent, while cutting lucrative trade deals with a gallery of rogue states and refusing to boost their defense budgets or take the other necessary steps to establish an independent foreign policy. Could China assume the role? It is ruled by a dictatorship, hobbled by a dysfunctional ideology, and it inspires only fear and loathing amongst its neighbors. The United Nations? Far from existing as an autonomous entity, the organization is nothing more than a collection of states, many of them autocratic and few of them as public-spirited as America—which, in any case, provides the U.N. with most of its financial, political and military muscle.

A humane future, then, will require an American foreign policy that is unapologetic, idealistic, assertive and well funded. America must not only be the world's policeman or its sheriff, it must be its beacon and guide. "A policeman gets his assignments from higher authority," writes foreign policy analyst Joshua Muravchik, "but in the community of nations there is no authority higher than America." This sentiment is not merely an assertion of national pride. It is simple fact. The alternative to American leadership is a chaotic, Hobbesian world where there is no authority to thwart aggression, ensure peace and security or enforce international norms. This is what it means to be a global superpower with global responsibilities. It is short-sighted to imagine that a policy of "humility" is either safer or less expensive than a policy that aims to preclude and deter the emergence of new threats, that has the United States arriving quickly at the scene of potential trouble before it has fully erupted, that addresses threats to the national interest before they develop into full-blown crises. Senator Kay Bailey Hutchison expressed a common but mistaken view when she wrote a few years ago that "a superpower is more credible and effective when it maintains a measured distance from all regional conflicts." In fact, this is precisely the way for a superpower to cease being a superpower.

Still, it is fair to ask how the rest of the world will respond to a prolonged period of American dominance. Charles A. Kupchan, author of *The End of the American Era: U.S. Foreign Policy and the Geopolitics of the Twenty-first Century,* cautions that the Bush doctrine's "neo-imperialist overtones" could foster "the very countervailing coalition that the administration says it is trying to avoid." To be sure, those regimes that find an American-led world order menacing to their existence will seek to cut away at American power, form tactical alliances with other rogue states for the common purpose of unsettling the international order, and look for ways to divide the United States from its allies. None of this, however, adds up to a convincing argument against American preeminence. The issue today is not American "arrogance." It is the inescapable reality of American power in all its many forms. Those who suggest that these international resentments could somehow be eliminated by a more restrained American foreign policy are deluding themselves. Even a United States that never again intervened in a place like Iraq would still find itself the target of jealousy, resentment and in some cases even fear. A more polite but still preeminently powerful United States would continue to stand in the way of Chinese ambitions, offend Islamists and grate on French insecurities. Unless the United States is prepared to divest itself of its real power and influence, thereby allowing other nations to achieve a position of relative parity on the world stage, would-be challengers as well as the envious will still have much to resent.

But it is doubtful that any effective grouping of nations is likely to emerge to challenge American power. Much of the current international attack against American "hegemonism" is posturing. Allies such as the French may cavil about the American "hyperpower," but they recognize the benefits that their dependence on the United States as the guarantor of international order brings them. As for Russia and China and the Islamic world, the prospect of effective joint action between these forces is slight. Their long history of mutual mistrust is compounded by the fact that they do not share common strategic goals—even with regard to the United States. The unwillingness of these and other powers to gang up on the United States also has much to do with the fact that it does not pursue a narrow, selfish definition of its national interest, but generally finds its interest in a benevolent international order.

Is the task of maintaining American primacy and making a consistent effort to shape the international environment beyond the capacity of Americans? Not if American leaders have the understanding and the political will to do what is necessary. What is required is not particularly forbidding. Indeed, much of the task ahead consists of building on already-existing strengths.

Despite its degradation during the 1990s, the United States still wields the strongest military forces in the world. It has demonstrated its prowess on several occasions since the end of the Cold War—in Panama, in Iraq, in Kosovo and in Afghanistan. Still, those victories owed their success to a legacy the United States has lived off for over a decade. It is true that despite increases in the latest Bush defense budget, the United States still spends too little on its military capabilities, in terms of both present readiness and investment in future weapons technologies. The gap between America's strategic ends and the means available to accomplish those ends is significant, a fact that becomes more evident each time the United States deploys forces abroad.

Still, the task of repairing these deficiencies and creating a force that can shape the international environment today, tomorrow and twenty years from now is manageable. It would probably require spending about $100 billion per year above current defense budgets. This price tag may seem daunting, but in historical terms it represents only a modest commitment of America's wealth. The sum is still low by the standards of the past fifty years, and far lower than most great powers have spent on their militaries throughout history. Is the aim of maintaining American primacy really not worth that much?

The United States also inherited from the Cold War a legacy of strong alliances in Europe and Asia, and with Israel in the Middle East. Those alliances are a bulwark of American power, and more important still, they comprise the heart of the liberal democratic order that the United States seeks to preserve and extend. Critics of a distinctly American internationalism often claim that it is unilateralist in its heart. In fact, a strategy aimed at preserving American preeminence would require an even greater U.S. commitment to its allies. The United States would not be merely an "offshore balancer" in actions of last resort, as many recommend. It would not be a "reluctant sheriff," rousing itself to action only when the threatened townsfolk turn to it in desperation. American preeminence cannot be maintained from a distance. The United States should instead conceive of itself as at once a European power, an Asian power and, of course, a Middle Eastern power. It would act as if threats to the interests of our allies are threats to us, which indeed they are. It would act as if the flouting of civilized rules of conduct are threats that affect us with almost the same immediacy as if they were occurring on our doorstep. To act otherwise would make the United States appear an unreliable partner in world affairs, and this would erode both American primacy and the international order itself.

A strong America capable of projecting force quickly and with devastating effect to important regions of the world would make it less likely that challengers to regional stability would attempt to alter the status quo in their favor. It might even deter such challengers from undertaking expensive efforts to arm themselves in the first place. An America whose willingness to project force is in doubt, on the other hand, can only encourage such challenges. The message we should be sending to potential foes is: "Don't even think about it." That kind of deterrence offers the best recipe for a lasting peace; it is much cheaper than fighting the wars that would follow should we fail to build such a capacity.

The ability to project force overseas, however, could increasingly be jeopardized over the coming years as smaller powers acquire weapons of mass destruction and the missiles to launch them at American forces, at our allies and at the American homeland. Oddly enough, foreign critics, who carp that missile defense will cement U.S. hegemony and make Americans "masters of the world," grasp its rationale better than critics here at home. The real rationale for missile defense is that without it, an adversary armed with long-range missiles can, as Robert Joseph, President Bush's counterproliferation specialist at the National Security Council, argues, "hold American and allied cities hostage and thereby deter us from intervention." In other words, missile defense is about preserving America's ability to wield power abroad.

No one could have predicted that Iraq would be the first test-case of the post–Cold War era, just as no one could have predicted that Berlin would be the first battlefield of the Cold War. Indeed, the test could just as easily have come elsewhere—in North Korea, the Taiwan Strait or the Golan Heights. But history has conspired to locate the first serious challenge of the twenty-first century in Iraq. The failure to defeat Saddam was a defining moment for the presidencies of George H. W. Bush and Bill Clinton. The question of what to do about Saddam is now a defining moment for George W. Bush. Having fallen short before, will the United States get the answer right this time? If the president responds to the challenge of Iraq with the policies and worldviews of his predecessors, he too will surely fail. If, however, President Bush succeeds in bringing about regime change in Iraq, he will set a historical precedent—for Iraq, which could become the first Arab democracy; for the United States, which will demonstrate to all the compatibility of its interests and its ideals; and for the world, which America will have made a safer and more just place.

The mission begins in Baghdad, but it does not end there. Were the United States to retreat after victory into complacency and self-absorption, as it did the last time it went to war in Iraq, new dangers would soon arise. Preventing this outcome will be a burden, of which war in Iraq represents but the first installment. But America cannot escape its responsibility for maintaining a decent world order. The answer to this challenge is the American idea itself, and behind it the unparalleled military and economic strength of its custodian. Duly armed, the United States can act to secure its safety and to advance the cause of liberty—in Baghdad and beyond.

Notes

Part One: Saddam's Tyranny

Chapter 1: Tyranny at Home

page

4 "Three Whom God Should Not Have Created": Judith Miller and Laurie Mylroie, *Saddam Hussein and the Crisis in the Gulf* (New York: Times Books, 1990), p. 38.

5 "We hanged spies": Miller and Mylroie, *Crisis in the Gulf,* p. 34.

6 "made him far more ruthless": Miller and Mylroie, *Crisis in the Gulf,* p. 35.

6 "To visit Iraq is to enter the land of big brother": Miller and Mylroie, *Crisis in the Gulf,* p. 24.

6 "The Baath have saddled Iraq": Kanan Makiya, *Republic of Fear* (Berkeley: University of California Press, 1998), p. 42.

7 "not more than one million Iraqis": An Iraqi quoted in Youssef Ibrahim, "Baghdad's Burden," *New York Times,* 25 October 1994.

7 "zero defects program": Kelly quoted in Louise Lief, "Even Three Sets of Spies Aren't Enough," *U.S. News and World Report,* 4 February 1991.

8 "family's home was bulldozed": Miller and Mylroie, *Crisis in the Gulf,* p. 50.

8 Man's tongue sliced off: see description in "Iraq: Systematic Torture of Political Prisoners," *Amnesty International,* August 2001, p. 10.

8 Iraq had more unresolved "disappearances": "Iraq and Kurdistan," *Human Rights Watch World Report,* 1998, p. 1.

8   "profiteering" and "Greedy Merchants": Makiya, *Republic of Fear,*
     p. xvi.

8f. Sexual torture of women by Iraqi government: Omar Ismael quoted
     in Marie Colvin, "Torturer Lays Bare Saddam's Death Machine," *Sun-
     day Times* (London), 14 January 2000; see also "Torture, Ill-Treatment,
     and Death in Iraq," *Amnesty International,* April 1989, pp. 250–53;
     "Human Rights in Iraq," *Middle East Watch,* November 1990, p. 248.

10   Mass killing at Abu Ghraib prison: defector quoted in Peter Beau-
     mont, "Saddam's Executioner Tells of Slaughter in Jail 'Cleansing,'"
     London Observer, 3 December 2000.

10   "eyes gouged out, fingernails missing": "Human Rights in Iraq,"
     Middle East Watch, November 1990, p. 248.

10   Torture of al-Sadr: Miller and Mylroie, *Crisis in the Gulf,* p. 108.

11   Shiite uprising and "killing fields": Sandra Mackey, *The Reckoning*
     (New York: Norton, 2002), pp. 289–91.

11   "wipe out" the local populations: "Saddam's Work in the Marsh-
     lands," *Wall Street Journal,* 19 August 1992.

11   "withdraw all foodstuffs": Mackey, *Reckoning,* p. 315.

11   "indiscriminate bombardments on civilian settlements" and Sad-
     dam's attack on the marsh Arabs: see *UN Human Rights Commission
     Special Report,* August 1992; "Saddam's Work in the Marshlands,"
     Wall Street Journal, 19 August 1992; David Rose, "Iraq's Arsenal of
     Terror," *Vanity Fair,* May 2002, pp. 120–31.

12   "a method to facilitate government control": *UN Human Rights Com-
     mission Special Report,* August 1992.

12   Killing of fish, turtles and other marsh life: damage to marshes as
     described in Shyam Bhattia, "Murder of the Marshes," *London
     Observer,* 28 February 1993.

12   "racist war of extermination" and the burning of women and chil-
     dren in Mosul: Makiya, *Republic of Fear,* pp. 22–23.

13   Left half of Iraq's Kurdish population homeless: *London Times,* quoted
     in Miller and Mylroie, *Crisis in the Gulf,* p. 52.

13   Account of Kurds fleeing during 1974 offense: Mackey, *Reckoning,*
     p. 224.

13   "I will kill them all with chemical weapons" and "mass executions"
     of Kurds: Jeffrey Goldberg, "The Great Terror," *New Yorker,* 3 March
     2002.

Chapter 2: Aggression Abroad

15 "let him rant and rave": Dick Armey quoted in Eric Schmitt, "Iraq Is Defiant as GOP Leader Opposes Attack," *New York Times,* 8 August 2002.

16 "Pyramids of skulls": "King Says Saddam's Policies Have Left Pyramids of Skulls," Associated Press, 15 December 1997.

16 "must be ranked as one of this century's worst strategic miscalculations": Michael Sterner, "The Persian Gulf: The Iran-Iraq War," *Foreign Affairs,* Fall 1984.

16 Saddam believed the war would be over within a month: Sandra Mackey, *The Reckoning* (New York: Norton, 2002), p. 252.

17 "Saddam's convoy was besieged by Iranian troops": Judith Miller and Laurie Mylroie, *Saddam Hussein and the Crisis in the Gulf* (New York: Times Books, 1990), p. 114.

17 "inept strategy and tactics of the Iraqis": account of Saddam's military incompetence in Makiya, *Republic of Fear,* pp. 276–77.

17 Iraq launched at least 189 Scud missiles at Teheran: Michael R. Gordon and Bernard E. Trainor, *The Generals' War* (Boston: Little, Brown and Co., 1995), p. 229.

17f. "We are frying them like eggplants": Mark Fineman, "Madness in the Marshes," *Los Angeles Times,* 14 August 1990.

18 "batons, truncheons, or wire cables": *Los Angeles Times,* 22 January 1991.

18 Testimony of Andrew Whitley: Quoted in Dana Priest, "Iraq Routinely Mistreated Iranian POWs," *Washington Post,* 25 January 1991.

18 Documented instances of Iraq using chemical weapons on Iranians: Jill Smolowe, "Chemical Warfare," *Time,* 22 August 1988.

18 Aziz openly admitted that Iraq had enshrined their use: Patrick Tyler, "UN Cites Iraqi Use of Toxic Gas," *Washington Post,* 2 August 1988.

18 "more intense and frequent use" of chemical weapons: Peter Spielman, "Security Council Condemns Chemical Attacks against Iranians," Associated Press, 27 August 1988.

19 Iraq bombarded Iran with chemical weapons for five consecutive years: account of Iraqi gas attacks in Patrick Tyler, "UN Cites Iraqi Use of Toxic Gas," *Washington Post,* 2 August 1988.

19 "pesticide to throw at these swarms of insects": William Drozdiak, "US Accuses Iraq of Employing Chemical Weapons against Iran," *Washington Post,* 6 March 1984.

20 Saddam's forces executed or tortured to death and "Electric shock was applied to sensitive parts of the body": John Lancaster, "Administration Releases Report on Iraqi War Crimes in Kuwait," *Washington Post,* 20 March 1993.

21 "Are you getting your milk and cornflakes too?": Michael Kranish, "Saddam Hussein on TV with Captives," *Boston Globe,* 24 August 1990.

21 Crippled 749 oil wells and the discharge of nearly eight million barrels of oil: "Gulf War Update," *Science News,* 16 November 1991.

21 "overcast skies drips a greasy black rain": Dowell and Riley, "A Man-Made Hell on Earth," *Time,* 3 March 1991.

22 "foul Jewish usurpers": Hussein speech as reported by the Iraqi News Agency, *BBC Worldwide,* 17 July 2001.

22 "confront Israel's existing bombs": Hussein speech on Baghdad Radio as reported in the *New York Times,* 24 July 1982.

23 Iraqi officials have stated explicitly that Iraq maintains biological weapons: Richard Butler, *The Greatest Threat* (New York: PublicAffairs, 2001), p. 118.

23 "the extinction of the Zionist entity": Miller and Mylroie, *Crisis in the Gulf,* p. 14.

23 Relatives of suicide bombers earn $25,000: Mohammed Daraghmeh, "Iraq Increases Payments to Families of Palestinian Suicide Bombers to $25,000," Associated Press, 3 April 2002.

23 "nearby town of Afula with a gun and opened fire": London's *Daily Telegraph* as quoted in *Vancouver Sun,* 30 May 2002.

23 "solid evidence of the presence in Iraq of Al Qaeda members": CIA director George Tenet letter to Sen. Bob Graham, chairman of the Senate Intelligence Committee, 9 October 2002.

24 Group was trained by Al Qaeda forces in Afghanistan: Daniel Eisenberg, " 'We're Taking Him Out,' " *Time,* 13 May 2002.

24 "In a vicious, repressive dictatorship": Donald Rumsfeld press briefing, Pentagon, 20 August 2002.

24 "We were convinced that money from Iraq": Stanley Bedlington

quoted in Peter Eisler, "Targeting Saddam: Was There an Iraqi 9/11 Link?" *USA Today,* 3 December 2001. See same article for Iraq using bin Laden to funnel money to Algerian terrorists.

24 "Iraq has provided training to Al Qaeda members": CIA director George Tenet letter to Sen. Bob Graham, chairman of the Senate Intelligence Committee, 9 October 2002.

25 "only Iraq would give safe haven to Abu Nidal": White House spokesman Ari Fleischer, press briefing, Crawford, Texas, 20 August 2002.

25 "Iraq provided bases to several terrorist groups": U.S. Department of State Report, "Patterns of Global Terrorism," 21 May 2002.

25 Hamas, too, has benefited from Saddam's generosity: David Rose, "Iraq's Arsenal of Terror," *Vanity Fair,* 2 May 2002.

25 "We were training these people to attack installations": Iraqi defector quoted in Chris Hedges, "Defectors Cite Iraqi Training for Terrorism," *New York Times,* 8 November 2001.

26 "They are even trained how to use utensils": Iraqi defector on Salman Pak quoted in Michael Dornheim, "Satellite Photos Believed to Show Airliner for Training Highjackers," *Aviation Week and Space Technology,* 7 January 2002.

Chapter 3: Weapons of Mass Destruction

27 "Predators of the twenty-first century": President Clinton, Pentagon, 17 February 1998.

27 Iraq began its efforts to develop biological weapons in 1973 or 1974 and conducted "research on microorganisms for military purposes": United Nations Report Annex C, "Status of Verification of Iraq's Biological Warfare Program" (hereafter Annex C), 25 January 1999, p. 37.

28 Saddam resolved to diversify the weapons of mass destruction: Judith Miller and Laurie Mylroie, *Saddam Hussein and the Crisis in the Gulf* (New York: Times Books, 1990), pp. 156–57.

28 Imported 819 long-range combat missiles: United Nations Report Annex A, "Status of the Material Balances in the Missile Area" (hereafter Annex A), 25 January 1999, p. 3.

28 "field tests of BW agents started in late 1987/early 1998": details of Iraq's BW program quoted in Annex C, p. 32.

28f. "design, component testing, and the construction of manufacturing facilities": David Kay, "Denial and Deception: The Lessons of Iraq," *U.S. Intelligence at the Crossroads: Agendas for Reform,* ed. Roy Godson, Gary James Schmitt and Ernest May (Washington, D.C.: Brassey's, 1995), p. 2.

29 "possessed nearly 10,000 nerve gas warheads": United Nations Report Annex B, "Status of the Verification of Iraq's Chemical Weapons Programme" (hereafter Annex B), 25 January 1999, p. 7.

29 Ten times the number of chemical weapons: David Kay, "With More at Stake, Less Will Be Verified," *Washington Post,* 17 November 2002.

29 "no mention was made of Aflatoxin": Annex C, pp. 9–10.

29 "significant documentary material and equipment": "Inspectors Charge Iraq Has Ongoing Nuclear Weapons Programme," *United Nations Chronicle,* December 1991.

30 "the equivalent of war in arms control": Rolf Ekeus quoted in Richard Butler, *The Greatest Threat* (New York: PublicAffairs, 2001), p. 53.

30 "'dog ate my homework'": Iraqi WMD concealment excuses found in Butler, *Greatest Threat,* p. 51.

30 "highest level of concealment-related decisions": United Nations Report Annex D, "Actions by Iraq to Obstruct Disarmament," 25 January 1999, p. 6.

30 "a truckers' picnic was taking place": Butler, *Greatest Threat,* p. 157.

30 France and Russia seized every opportunity: Lawrence F. Kaplan, "Bluffing: Why Is Bush Demanding Weapons Inspectors?" *New Republic,* 25 February 2002, p. 19.

31 "a man I can do business with": Kofi Annan quoted in Robin Wright, "UN Chief Confidant about Pact with Iraq," *Los Angeles Times,* 25 February 1998.

31 "more aligned with the rest of the U.N. system": Kaplan, "Bluffing: Why Is Bush Demanding Weapons Inspectors?"

32 "same old game of hide and seek" and "salami-slicing": Kaplan, "Bluffing: Why Is Bush Demanding Weapons Inspectors?"

32 Weapons inspectors could never locate: list of unaccounted-for weapons quoted in Judith Miller and William J. Broad, "Germs, Atoms and Poison Gas: The Iraqi Shell Game," *New York Times,* 20 December 1998.

32 "they've lied across the board": Scott Ritter, testimony before the Senate Armed Services Committee, 3 September 1998.

32   "Iraq is well into CW production": Richard Butler, testimony before the Senate Foreign Relations Committee, 31 July 2002.

32f.   "reinitiate both its CW and BW programs": Central Intelligence Agency, "Unclassified Report to Congress on the Acquisition of Technology Related to Weapons of Mass Destruction and Advanced Conventional Munitions," February 2000.

33   Cohen released a Pentagon report: Myers and Schmitt, "Iraq Rebuilt Weapon Factories, US Officials Say," *New York Times,* 22 January 2001.

33   "Mr. Saeed said that several of the production": Judith Miller, "Iraqi Tells of Renovations at Sites for Chemical and Nuclear Arms," *New York Times,* 20 December 2001.

33   Bush administration and British government presented further evidence: White House Background Document, "A Decade of Deception and Defiance," 12 September 2002; The Assessment of the British Government, "Iraq's Weapons of Mass Destruction," 24 September 2002.

Part Two: The American Response

Chapter 4: Narrow Realism (Bush I)

39   "It is too bad they both can't lose": Norman Kempster, "US Favors Iraq in War, Shultz Indicates," *Los Angeles Times,* 17 December 1986, p. 22.

39   "Eximbank could play a crucial role": Bruce W. Jentleson, *With Friends Like These: Reagan, Bush and Saddam, 1982–1990* (New York: Simon and Schuster, 1994), p. 43.

39   "encourage other countries to arm and finance Iraq's war effort": Jentleson, *With Friends Like These,* p. 45.

40   "set aside the emotions of the moment": Jentleson, *With Friends Like These,* p. 84.

41   "a more responsible, status-quo state": Jentleson, *With Friends Like These,* p. 98.

41   "demand of Iraq what we do of its neighbors": Jentleson, *With Friends Like These,* p. 104.

41f.   "It is in no way [U.S.] policy": Jentleson, *With Friends Like These,* p. 146.

42 "I believe your problem is with the Western media": Jentleson, *With Friends Like These,* p. 146.

43 "saw the presidential message": Michael R. Gordon and Bernard E. Trainor, *The Generals' War: The Inside Story of the Conflict in the Gulf* (Boston: Little, Brown and Co., 1995), p. 23.

43 "Let me assure you": Gordon and Trainor, *The Generals' War,* p. 23.

43 "I know personally": R. W. Apple Jr., "Noncandidate Powell Stirs Waves on Republican Right," *New York Times,* 3 October 1995.

43 "The American people do not want their young dying": Gordon and Trainor, *The Generals' War,* p. 33.

43 "The vaunted Republican Guard formations": Rick Atkinson, *Crusade: The Untold Story of the Persian Gulf War* (Boston: Houghton Mifflin, 1993), p. 470.

44 "We have done the job": Gordon and Trainor, *The Generals' War,* p. 416.

44 "We would be committing ourselves": George H. W. Bush and Brent Scowcroft, *A World Transformed,* paperback edition (New York: Vintage Books, 1999), p. 433.

44 "It would not contribute": Colin Powell, *My American Journey,* paperback edition (New York: Random House, 1996), p. 512.

44 "our practical intention": Powell, *My American Journey,* p. 516.

44 "I envisioned a postwar government": Brent Scowcroft, interview with *ABC News,* 7 February 1998.

45 "the Iraqi people to take matters into their own hands": President George H. W. Bush, remarks to the American Association for the Advancement of Science, 15 February 1991.

45 "if Saddam had fallen": Powell, *My American Journey,* p. 513.

46 "goes not abroad, in search of monsters": John Quincy Adams, Fourth of July Address, 1821.

46 "phenomenon of the moral crusade": Hans J. Morgenthau, *In Defense of the National Interest* (New York: Alfred A. Knopf, 1951), p. 35.

47 "restraint in the uses of power": Quoted in Robert Kagan, "The Revisionist," *New Republic,* 21 June 1999, p. 36.

47 "I was skeptical about the wisdom": Bush and Scowcroft, *A World Transformed,* p. 188.

48 "painful to watch Yeltsin": Bush and Scowcroft, *A World Transformed,* p. 556.

48 "not support those who seek independence": President George H. W. Bush, remarks to the Supreme Soviet of the Republic of the Ukraine, 1 August 1991.

48 "nothing that I really want China to do": Bush and Scowcroft, *A World Transformed*, p. 111.

48 "Following the Gulf War": David Gompert, "How to Defeat Serbia," *Foreign Affairs*, July/August 1994, p. 30.

49 "We don't have a dog in that fight": James Baker, quoted in *Time*, 17 August 1992.

Chapter 5: Wishful Liberalism (Clinton)

50 "left the Kurds and the Shiites": President Bill Clinton, interview with *New York Times*, 28 June 1992.

50 "will not turn our backs": Al Gore, quoted in Scott MacLeod, "Gore to Rebels: We're with You, Maybe," *Time*, 11 August 1997.

50 "Our purpose is deliberate": Martin Indyk, remarks to the Washington Institute for Near East Policy, 18 May 1993.

50 "the United States will not support this": *ABC News*, 7 February 1998.

51 "These guys are a feckless bunch": Robin Wright, "Jordan King Aims to Organize Foes of Saddam Hussein," *Los Angeles Times*, 7 December 1995.

51 "They are really more gnats": John Lancaster and David B. Ottaway, "With CIA's Help, Group in Jordan Targets Saddam," *Washington Post*, 23 June 1996.

51 "Our interest in the Kurds": William Perry on *NewsHour with Jim Lehrer*, 17 September 1996.

51 "Our missiles sent the following": President Bill Clinton, address from the Oval Office, 3 September 1996.

51 "a message directed at Iraq": Madeleine Albright on *NewsHour with Jim Lehrer*, 28 June 1993.

51 "It was not designed": Al Gore, interview with *CBS News*, 28 June 1993.

52 "a devastating blow": Al Gore, quoted in Susan Bennett and Frank Greve, "A Question of Deterrence," *Houston Chronicle*, 29 June 1993.

53 "we are not talking about a war": Madeleine Albright, remarks at Tennessee State University, 19 February 1998.

53f. Finally, in December 1998: Lawrence F. Kaplan, "Rollback," *New Republic,* 30 September 2000.

54 "predicted fierce and effective Iraqi resistance": Jim Hoagland, "Virtual Policy," *Washington Post,* 7 March 1999.

54 "stopped trying to convince anyone": Kenneth M. Pollack, *The Threatening Storm: The Case for Invading Iraq* (New York: Random House, 2002), p. 102.

54 "we know that they represent fighters": Kaplan, "Rollback."

55 "The guidance equipment is still there": Selean Hacaoglu, "U.S. Air Force Using Cement Bombs against Iraq," Associated Press, 7 October 1999.

55 "During a conversation": Pollack, *Threatening Storm,* p. 99.

56 "this might create a climate": Colum Lynch, "UN Arms Inspectors Back Down," *Washington Post,* 31 August 2000.

57 This reflexive suspicion of American power: Lawrence F. Kaplan, "Trading Places," *New Republic,* 23 October 2000.

58 "we simply don't have the leverage": Peter Tarnoff quoted in *Newsday,* 30 May 1993.

59 "We've simply got to focus on rebuilding": President Bill Clinton quoted in the *Washington Post,* 17 October 1993.

59 "we are really powerless": William Perry, interview on *Meet the Press,* 27 November 1994.

59 "The forces of global integration": President Bill Clinton, remarks to the United Nations, 22 September 1997.

60 "from the floor of the stock exchange": Strobe Talbott, "Globalization and Diplomacy," *Foreign Policy,* September 1997, p. 68.

60 "If the American people don't know anything": President Bill Clinton, remarks to the American Federation of State, County and Municipal Employees Conference, 23 March 1999.

60 "a humanitarian crisis a long way from home": Warren Christopher quoted in James Chace, "Exit, NATO," *New York Times,* 4 June 1993.

60 "This agreement will help": President Bill Clinton, statement regarding U.S.–North Korea Framework Agreement, 18 October 1994.

61 "long reach of our nation's": Madeleine Albright, news conference on the bombings of the U.S. embassies in Kenya and Tanzania, 27 August 1998.

Chapter 6: A Distinctly American Internationalism (Bush II)

64 "From the outset of our existence": Robert W. Tucker, "Exemplar or Crusader?" *National Interest,* Fall 1986, p. 69.

65 "not as the problem-solver of the world": Richard Barnet quoted in John Ehrman, *The Rise of Neoconservatism: Intellectuals and Foreign Affairs, 1945–1994* (New Haven: Yale University Press, 1995), p. 27.

66 "the objective of any American administration": Richard Nixon quoted in Jeffrey Record, *Making War, Thinking History: Munich, Vietnam and Presidential Uses of Force from Korea to Kosovo* (Annapolis: Naval Institute Press, 2002), p. 76.

68 "too quick to reach out": Stephen Hadley, interview with National Public Radio, 13 September 2000.

68 "a return to professionalism": Jonathan Clarke, "May Powell Win the G.O.P. Slug Fest over Foreign Policy," *Los Angeles Times,* 6 February 2001, p. 9.

69 "deep ethnic and religious roots": Colin Powell, "Why Generals Get Nervous," *New York Times,* 8 October 1992, p. 35.

69 "order is more fundamental": Richard Haass, "What to Do with American Primacy," *Foreign Affairs,* September/October 1999, p. 37.

69 "even though the world would be far better off": Richard Haass quoted in Lawrence F. Kaplan, "Drill Sergeant," *New Republic,* 26 March 2001, p. 17.

70 "What's the point": Colin Powell, *My American Journey,* paperback edition (New York: Random House, 1996), p. 561.

71 "This significant step": Colin Powell quoted in *Washington Post,* 15 May 2002.

72 "The advance of human freedom": President George W. Bush, address to Congress, 20 September 2002.

72 "the application of power": "The Limits of Power," *New York Times,* 31 January 2002.

73 "While there are many dangers": President George W. Bush, remarks at the Cincinnati Museum Center, 7 October 2002.

74 "take the battle to the enemy": President George W. Bush, commencement address, United States Military Academy, 1 June 2002.

75 "dissuade potential adversaries": *National Security Strategy of the United States, 2002,* 17 September 2002.

Part Three: America's Mission

Chapter 7: From Deterrence to Preemption

79 "Given the goals of rogue states and terrorists": *National Security Strategy of the United States, 2002,* 17 September 2002.

79 "there are some even today who say": Senator Tom Harkin, remarks to the Senate, 4 January 1991.

80 "keep Iraq in its box": Madeleine Albright on *Moneyline,* CNN, 13 September 2002.

80 "Containment is so far working": Senator Carl Levin on *Meet the Press,* ABC, 12 August 2002.

80 "there is no current danger to the United States": Jimmy Carter, "The Troubling New Face of America," *Washington Post,* 5 September 2002.

80 "containment is not the answer": Richard Butler, remarks before the Senate Foreign Relations Committee, 31 July 2002.

80 "is closing down possibly within the next 2–3 years": Khidir Hamza, remarks before the Senate Foreign Relations Committee, 31 July 2002.

80 "The argument comes down to this": Vice President Cheney, remarks to the Veterans of Foreign Wars in Nashville, Tennessee, 26 August 2002.

81 "an Iraq carried forward under this regime": Charles Duelfer on *Talk of the Nation,* National Public Radio, 8 August 2002.

81 "Threatening to use [his] weapons for blackmail": Brent Scowcroft, "Don't Attack Saddam," *Wall Street Journal,* 15 August 2002.

81 "We don't have to wonder if he can be deterred": Steve Chapman, "Case for Invading Iraq Is Full of Holes," *Baltimore Sun,* 3 September 2002.

82 "Iraqi arrogance—which afflicted both Saddam and his generals": U.S. Air Force, *The Gulf War Air Power Survey,* vol. 1, *Planning and Command and Control* (Washington, D.C.: U.S. Government Printing Office, 1993), p. 81.

82 "If we cannot fully understand the acts of other people": Walter Lippmann, *Public Opinion* (New York: MacMillan, 1927), p. 85.

82 "state of mind—his self-interest, his sanity": Jonathan Schell quoted in Lawrence Kaplan, "Offensive Line," *New Republic,* 12 March 2001.

83 "why it is necessary for us to bomb": Mary McGrory, "Unequal Opportunity for Tyrants," *Washington Post,* 20 October 2002.

83 "the intelligence community can provide the necessary warning": Henry Shelton, letter to Senator James Inhofe, 24 August 1998.

84 "The probability that a missile armed with weapons of mass destruction": National Intelligence Council Report, *Foreign Missile Developments and Ballistic Missile Threat to the Uniied States through 2015,* 2000.

84 "barely plausible when there was only one nuclear opponent": Henry Kissinger, "Ready for Revitalizing," *Washington Post,* 9 March 1995, p. A21.

85 "in a small number of cases": Colin Powell, remarks before the Senate Foreign Relations Committee, 26 September 2002.

85 "Preemption ... runs completely against U.S. political and strategic culture": Frank Hoffman quoted in Thomas E. Ricks and Vernon Loeb, "Bush Developing Military Policy of Striking First," 10 June 2002.

85 "would not be consistent": Dick Armey quoted by Eric Schmitt, "Iraq Is Defiant as G.O.P. Leader Opposes Attack," *New York Times,* 9 August 2002, p. A6.

85 "What this doctrine does is to destroy": Al Gore, remarks at the Commonwealth Club, San Francisco, 23 September 2002.

85 "the right of every sovereign state to protect": Secretary of State Elihu Root quoted by Ruth Wedgwood in "Six Degrees of Preemption," *Washington Post,* 29 September 2002, p. B2.

86 "Nor need a would-be victim nation wait": Richard Regan, *Just War* (Washington, D.C.: The Catholic University of America Press, 1996), p. 51.

86 "Potential victims cannot wait": Kissinger, *Washington Post,* 10 December 2002, p. A29.

87 "Preemption as intervention": Robert Killebrew quoted in "Six Degrees of Preemption," *Washington Post,* 29 September 2002, p. B2.

88 "Forward engagement means addressing problems": *2000 Democratic Party Platform,* 15 August 2000.

88 "the developing norm in favour of intervention": Kofi Annan, "Two Concepts of Sovereignty," *The Economist,* 18 September 1999.

88 "What you are seeing in this administration": Richard Haass quoted

in Nicholas Lemann, "The Next World Order," *New Yorker*, 1 April 2002, p. 42.

88 "Israel's sneak attack on a French-built nuclear reactor": "Israel's Illusion," *New York Times*, 9 June 1981, p. A14.

88 "We under no circumstances will allow an enemy": Israeli government statement about the attack against the Iraqi nuclear reactor, 8 June 1981.

89 "History's judgment should inform our own judgment today": Benjamin Netanyahu, remarks before the Senate Foreign Relations Committee, 14 September 2002.

89 "History is littered with cases of inaction": Condoleezza Rice, BBC Radio 4, 15 August 2002.

89 "I believe any action in Iraq at this time": Dianne Feinstein, remarks to the 107th Congress, 5 September 2002.

89 "very, very dire consequences": Tom Daschle, remarks to reporters, 3 September 2002.

89 "In all the years I have seen": King Abdullah of Jordan quoted in Glenn Kessler and Peter Slavin, "Abdullah: Foreign Leaders Oppose Attack; Jordanian King to Urge Bush to Focus on Peace in Mideast, Not Invasion of Iraq," *Washington Post*, 1 August 2002, p. A24.

89 "Germany will not participate": Gerhard Schroeder, ARD Television, 10 August 2002.

89 "we have to follow the United Nations": Jean Chretien, remarks to President Bush in Detroit, 10 September 2002.

90 "faced a simple choice": Richard Holbrooke, "Give Diplomacy More Time," *Washington Post*, 7 September 2002, p. A17.

90 "may emerge as greater than the sum": Boutros Boutros-Ghali quoted in Joshua Muravchik, *The Imperative of American Leadership* (Washington, D.C.: AEI Press, 1991), p. 82.

90 "There is nothing wrong with the Charter": Quoted in Muravchik, *The Imperative of American Leadership*, p. 78.

91 "In fact, even as [Prime Minister] Chirac was proclaiming the sanctity": "Let the U.N. Vote," *Washington Post*, 23 October 2002.

91 "France and Russia have turned the United Nations": Fareed Zakaria, "The Lonesome Doves of Europe," *Newsweek*, 30 September 2002.

91 "open the gates of hell in the Middle East": Arab League Secretary General Amr Moussa, 5 September 2002.

93 "being so eager to oppose Bush": Salman Rushdie, "A Liberal Argument for Regime Change," *Washington Post,* 1 November 2002.

93 "the utopian nihilism of a left": David Rieff, *World Policy Journal,* 22 June 1999.

93 "Instead of internationalism, we find among the left": Christopher Hitchens, *Washington Post,* 20 October 2002.

93 "a constructive source of restraint": Stanley Hoffman, "America Alone in the World," *American Prospect,* 23 September 2002, p. 20.

93 "multilateralism is the isolationism of the internationalist": Charles Krauthammer, "Alone at the Top," *Commercial Appeal,* 21 July 1991, p. B4.

93f. "The crucial difference between the Democratic establishment's support": Will Marshall quoted in Lawrence Kaplan, "On Iraq, McGovernism Returns," *New Republic,* 28 January 2002.

94 "obviously, U.S. national security is not at stake": Michael Walzer quoted in Lawrence Kaplan, "Meanwhile on the Left . . . ," *National Interest,* Spring 2000.

94 "the important question is not whether other countries": Editorial, *New Republic,* 23 September 2002.

Chapter 8: From Containment to Regime Change

95 "champion the cause of human dignity": *National Security Strategy of the United States, 2002,* 17 September 2002.

95 "Liberty for the Iraqi people": President George W. Bush in a speech in Cincinnati, 7 October 2002.

96 "It would not contribute to the stability": Colin Powell, *My American Journey,* paperback edition (New York: Random House, 1996), p. 512.

96 "Dire consequences would be the effect": Brent Scowcroft, "Don't Attack Saddam," *Wall Street Journal,* 15 August 2002, p. 12.

96 "morass": Lawrence Eagleburger on *Meet the Press,* NBC, 1 September 2002.

96 "how we are going to deal": Lawrence Eagleburger on *Crossfire,* CNN, 19 August 2002.

96 "What comes after a military invasion?": Senator Chuck Hagel on *This Week,* ABC, 1 September 2002.

97   "the overwhelming majority of the population": Phebe Marr, remarks to the Senate Foreign Relations Committee, 1 August 2002.

97   "we will not have a civil war in Iraq": Rend Rahim Francke, remarks to the Senate Foreign Relations Committee, 1 August 2002.

97   "One way to reconcile territorial integrity": Michael Mandelbaum, "U.S. Must Plan Post–Hussein Iraq," *Newsday,* 1 August 2002, p. A37.

98   "The President looked forward to a day": Michael Elliot, "The Lessons of Empire: As Bush Considers Colonizing Iraq, He Ought to Look at the Last Attempt," *Time,* 7 October 2002, p. 38.

98   "Democracy cannot be imposed": Shibley Telhami, "A Hidden Cost of War on Iraq," *New York Times,* 7 October 2002, p. A19.

99   "create a constitution assembly": Laith Kubba, "How to Achieve Democracy in Iraq," *Financial Times,* 7 October 2002, p. 13.

99   "a government that is democratic and pluralistic": Vice President Dick Cheney, remarks to the Veterans of Foreign Wars in Nashville, Tennessee, 26 August 2002.

99   "what the Arab world desperately needs": Thomas Friedman, "Iraq Debate Is Upside Down: America Has More to Fear from Angry Radicals with Nothing to Lose," *New York Times,* 19 September 2002, p. A18.

99   "prove to be as large as anything": Kanan Makiya, "The Day After: Planning for a Post-Saddam Iraq," remarks at a conference at the American Enterprise Institute, 3 October 2002.

100   "unlikely to change the contemporary Arab view": Adam Garfinkle, "The Impossible Imperative? Conjuring Arab Democracy," *National Interest,* Fall 2002.

100   "desert democracy where people read the Federalist Papers": Powell, *My American Journey,* p. 513.

100   "from imported western modules of 'instant democracy' ": Graham Fuller, "The Future of Political Islam," *Foreign Affairs,* March/April 2002, p. 48.

100   "I doubt that democracy U.S.-style can be exported": Howard Wiarda, "Can Democracy Be Exported? The Quest for Democracy in the United States Latin Policy," paper prepared for the Inter-American Dialogue on United States-Latin American Relations in the 1980s, sponsored by the Latin America Program of the Woodrow Wilson International Center for Scholars, Washington, D.C., March 1983.

100 "the best we can hope for is a constitutional monarchy": Joseph Grew quoted in Joshua Muravchik, *Exporting Democracy* (Washington, D.C.: AEI Press, 1991), p. 71.

101 "is not realistic in the Muslim world": Paula Dobriansky, speech to the Heritage Foundation, "The Diplomatic Front of the War on Terrorism: Can the Promotion of Democracy and Human Rights Tip the Scales?" 21 December 2001.

101 "the peoples of the Islamic nations want and deserve": President George W. Bush, speech at West Point Military Academy, 1 June 2002.

101 "I detect a dangerous arrogance": Senator Chuck Hagel quoted in James Kitfield, "The New New World Order," *National Journal,* 2 November 2002.

102 "The intersection of radicalism with technology": John Lewis Gaddis, "A Grand Strategy of Transformation," *Foreign Policy,* 1 November 2002.

102 "moderate Arab states would provide": Martin Indyk, "Long War in the Making," *Foreign Affairs,* January/February 2002, p. 75.

103 "suffer the fate of the Shah of Iran": Saudi Crown Prince Abdullah bin Abdul Aziz Al Saud, letter to President Bush, 28 October 2001.

103 "We reject the condescending view": Condoleezza Rice, Wriston Lecture, 1 October 2002.

103 "will use this moment of opportunity": *National Security Strategy,* 2002.

103f. "The United States possesses unprecedented": President Bush, speech at U.S. Military Academy at West Point, 1 June 2002.

104 "No people on earth yearn to be oppressed": *National Security Strategy,* 2002.

104 "balance of power that favors freedom": *National Security Strategy,* 2002.

104 "Cast in these terms, Muslims and Christians": Michael McFaul, "The Liberty Doctrine: Reclaiming the Purpose of American Power," *Policy Review,* 1 April 2002, p. 3.

105 "[When] the consent of the citizens": Immanuel Kant quoted in Michael U. Doyle, "Liberalism and War Politics," *American Political Science Review,* vol. 80, no. 4, pp. 1151–69.

105 "is a strategy based on the very realistic view": G. John Ikenberry, "Why Export Democracy?" *Wilson Quarterly,* 22 March 1999, p. 56.

107 "democratic government in a place that has never known one":
Leon Fuerth, "Intoxicated with Power," *Washington Post,* 16 October 2002, p. A25.

107 "that most dangerous breed of men, utopians": Anthony Lewis,
"Bush and Iraq," *New York Review of Books,* 7 November 2002.

107 "countries that have no past experience of democracy": Stanley
Hoffman, "America Alone in the World," *American Prospect,* 23 September 2002, p. 20.

107 "The Cold War led us astray": Joseph Duffey quoted in an interview
with Dick Kirschten, "Restive Relic," *National Journal,* 22 April 1995,
p. 976.

107 "forces beyond our control will have the most": George McGovern,
quoted in John Ehrman, *The Rise of Neoconservatism* (New Haven
and London: Yale University Press, 1995), p. 59.

107 "an age in which technology and electronics": Zbigniew Brzezinski, quoted in Ehrman, *The Rise of Neoconservatism,* p. 30.

108 "the fellow travelers of the new global economy": Sandy Berger,
speech to the Council on Foreign Relations: "Building a New Consensus on China," 6 June 1997.

108 "a force for change in China": President Bill Clinton, speech on
nuclear testing, 3 June 1998.

108 "The Chinese case destroys the American pretension": editorial, *Le
Monde,* quoted in Craig R. Whitney, "Dissents on Iran and Iraq,"
New York Times, 9 November 1997, p. D1.

109 "American power and leadership have been more responsible":
Christopher Patten, quoted in G. John Ikenberry, "The West: Precious, Not Unique," *Wilson Quarterly,* 22 March 1997, p. 162.

109 "The Communist leaders say, 'Don't interfere'": Alexandr Solzhenitsyn, *Warming to the West* (New York: Farrar, Straus and Giroux,
1976), p. 48.

109 "we are still inclined to pretend": Reinhold Niebuhr, *The Children
of Light and the Children of Darkness* (New York: Charles Scribner's
Sons, 1960; reprint, 1994), p. ix.

110 "one of those prehistoric monsters": George Kennan, quoted in
Robert Kagan, "American Power—A Guide for the Perplexed: Foreign Policy and U.S. Intervention in Foreign Conflicts," *Commentary,* April 1996.

110 "have a special interest in the development": Samuel Huntington quoted in Lawrence Kaplan, "Fall Guys," *New Republic,* 26 June 2000.

111 "The assumption that our values are universal": Robert F. Ellsworth and Dimitri K. Simes, "Imposing Our 'Values' by Force," *Washington Post,* 29 December 1999.

Chapter 9: From Ambivalence to Leadership

112 "surpassing, or equaling, the power of the United States": President George W. Bush, "The Bush Doctrine," speech to a joint session of Congress, 20 September 2001.

112 "The vision laid out in the Bush document": Hendrik Hertzberg, "Manifesto," *New Yorker,* 14 October 2002.

112 "The Bush administration has clearly broken": Frances Fitzgerald, "George Bush and the World," *New York Review of Books,* 26 September 2002.

112 "requirements of freedom apply fully": President George W. Bush, speech at the U.S. Military Academy at West Point, 1 June 2002.

113 "[T]his is a period not just of grave danger": Condoleezza Rice, speech to Johns Hopkins School of Advanced International Studies, 29 April 2002.

113 "America must be the dominant power": James Forrestal quoted in David Fromkin, *In the Time of the Americans* (New York: Alfred A. Knopf, 1995).

114 "international moral order": Henry Luce, quoted in William Kristol and Robert Kagan, *Present Dangers* (San Francisco: Encounter Books, 2000), p. 10.

114 "The American president and his key advisers": John Lewis Gaddis, *We Now Know: Rethinking Cold War History* (Oxford: Clarendon Press, 1997), p. 12.

114 "one of the most powerful forces for good": President Harry Truman, "Address before a Joint Session of the Congress, April 16, 1945," *Public Papers of the Presidents of the United States: Harry Truman, 1945* (Washington, D.C.: U.S. Government Printing Office, 1962), p. 6.

115 "Hitler had indicated what he intended to do": Donald Rumsfeld, interview on *Fox Special Report with Brit Hume,* 19 August 2002.

116 "Rumsfeld is a product of a time and generation": Evan Thomas, "Rumsfeld's War," *Newsweek,* 16 September 2002, p. 20.

116 "it is always 1968, the dark night": Noemie Emery, "Quagmire Nostalgia," *Weekly Standard,* 11 November 2002.

116 "Bosnia was not Vietnam": Richard Holbrooke, *To End a War* (New York: Random House, 1998), p. 118.

116 "I kept thinking of one thing: Vietnam": Anthony Lewis, "Bush and Iraq," *New York Review of Books,* 7 November 2002.

116 "learned from Vietnam": President George H. W. Bush, quoted in Jeffrey Record, *Making War, Thinking History: Munich, Vietnam and Presidential Uses of Force from Korea to Kosovo* (Annapolis: Naval Institute Press, 2002), p. 104.

116 "we've kicked the Vietnam syndrome": President George H. W. Bush, 1 March 1991.

116 "We've lived through that once already": President George H. W. Bush, ceremony marking the 50th anniversary of the start of the battle of Guadalcanal, 7 August 1992.

117 "remember the lessons of Vietnam": President George W. Bush, acceptance speech for the Republican nomination, 4 August 2000.

117 "Vietnam has become the defense establishment's morality play": Eliot Cohen, "Enough Blame to Go Round," *National Interest,* Spring 1998.

117 "In none of these recent foreign crises": Colin Powell, *My American Journey,* paperback edition (New York: Random House, 1996), p. 589.

117 "interfere in the internal affairs": President Jimmy Carter, address to the American Chamber of Commerce in Tokyo, 28 May 1975, quoted in Robert Kagan, *A Twilight Struggle: American Power in Nicaragua, 1977–1990* (New York: The Free Press, 1996), p. 51.

118f. "We no longer have the luxury": Michele Flournoy, quoted in "Terrorist Strikes Bring 'Homeland Defense' to Forefront," Associated Press, 16 September 2001.

119 "America has no empire to extend": President George W. Bush, speech at the U.S. Military Academy at West Point, 1 June 2002.

121 "A policeman gets his assignments": Joshua Muravchik, *The Imperative of American Leadership* (Washington, D.C.: AEI Press, 1991), p. 1.

121 "a superpower is more credible": Senator Kay Bailey Hutchison, "The Case for Strategic Sense," *Washington Post,* 13 September 1999, p. A27.

121 "the very countervailing coalition": Charles A. Kupchan quoted in Judith Miller, "Keeping U.S. No. 1," *New York Times*, 26 October 2002, p. B5.

124 "hold American and allied cities hostage": Robert Joseph, statement to the House Armed Services Committee, 28 June 2000.

Index